ECONOMIC FABLES

Ariel Rubinstein is Professor of Economics at Tel Aviv University and New York University. His books include *Bargaining and Markets* (with Martin J. Osborne, 1990), *A Course in Game Theory* (with Martin J. Osborne, 1994), *Modeling Bounded Rationality* (1998), *Economics and Language* (2000) and *Lecture Notes in Microeconomic Theory: The Economic Agent* (2005). He is a member of the Israel Academy of Sciences, a Foreign Honorary Member of the American Academy of Arts and Sciences and a Fellow and former President of the Econometric Society.

Economic Fables

Ariel Rubinstein

OpenBook
Publishers

Open Book Publishers CIC Ltd.,
40 Devonshire Road, Cambridge, CB1 2BL, United Kingdom
http://www.openbookpublishers.com

As with all Open Book Publishers titles, digital material and resources associated with this volume are available from our website:

http://www.openbookpublishers.com/product/136

ISBN Paperback: 978-1-906924-77-5
ISBN Digital (pdf): 978-1-906924-79-9
ISBN Digital ebook (epub version): 978-1-906924-80-5
ISBN Digital ebook (mobi version): 978-1-906924-81-2

This book was first published in Hebrew as *Agadot Hakalkala* (Kineret: Zemorah-Bitan, 2009).

Cover Image © Ariel Rubinstein

Typesetting by www.bookgenie.in

All paper used by Open Book Publishers is SFI (Sustainable Forestry Initiative), PEFC (Programme for the Endorsement of Forest Certification Schemes) and Forest Stewardship Council (FSC) certified.

Printed in the United Kingdom and United States by
Lightning Source for Open Book Publishers

Contents

Online Resources

The author has created a website containing interactive questions and games relating to various chapters in this book which is available to readers at:

http://www.openbookpublishers.com/exsites/136

It is recommended (though definitely not required) that you visit the site before reading the book.

0. Introduction

Bookkeeping with my father

I sat that evening in the back of the auditorium where the first Senate session of the academic year was being held. The table on the stage was draped with a green tablecloth that reached the floor. Seated at the table were the patricians of the university, which is situated north of an almost dry riverbed. A microphone was connected to scratchy loudspeakers. The national flag and the university flag drooped side by side in their stands.

The meeting opened with a string quartet whose young members had been asked to perform a classical piece to reflect the aesthetic taste of the Senate members, devotees of culture at a prestigious university. The rector then welcomed the participants, wishing them a year of fruitful research, a year of striving for excellence, and a year of peace. He noted a number of new programs at the university, "all of which express our pursuit of excellence." He went on to list the promotions, prizes and honors that members of the Senate had received during the summer months. Each honoree, when his name was mentioned, stood and made a slight bow, to the bored applause of a few of the more enthusiastic members of the Senate.

The Senate then discussed the appointment of members of a committee set up to examine ways of promoting excellence at the university. One by one, the candidates were introduced and their unique qualities cited. There was an occasional burst of erudite chuckling in the auditorium when one of the presenters strayed from his written recitation and inserted a witty remark in the chronicle of the candidate's meritorious deeds. The restraint disappeared when it came to female candidates. The first to leave the meeting had already begun to sneak out. And since to reach the exit they had to cross in front of the stage, they had no choice but to render an apologetic nod toward the self-satisfied rector.

Until that evening, I had never spoken before the Senate. During the meetings, I actually thought that I had a lot to say. I sometimes felt compelled to jot down an outline of profound, daring and provocative points I would raise in response to the outrageous statements, full of pathos, being voiced there. I would write these things on the back of an ATM receipt I found in my wallet, in handwriting that even I had trouble deciphering. But at the end of the meeting, I would toss the note in the trashcan outside the auditorium. And if for some reason the note remained in my pocket and I found it the next day, I would praise myself for being smart enough to refrain from publicly expressing the ridiculous things I had wanted so much to say just the day before.

The next item on the agenda was not supposed to dampen the festive atmosphere of the opening session. The administration proposed upgrading the program of studies in accounting to a status previously reserved only for main academic fields, and allowing the best students to receive a bachelor's degree after studying only accounting. The head of the accounting department extolled the virtues of the new program, his description easily covering a whole page, embellished by numerous tributes to excellence: the excellence of the lecturers, the excellence of the students – past, present, and particularly, future. The rector thanked the speaker for his fascinating remarks, and almost routinely began to take a formal vote when, from the back of the auditorium, I raised my hand and asked for permission to speak.

I approached the podium, with the pages of the speech I planned to deliver in my hand – three documents pertaining to the program and another small page, hiding between the folded pages. It was a photocopy of the diploma from a bookkeeping course offered at one of the evening classes of the Daughters of Zion in Bialystock. I had found the diploma in my father's forbidden drawer, under the compartment of the starched sheets and above the compartment of the embroidered tablecloths, along with his immigration certificate, his officer ranks from the Civil Defense unit, and a booklet of unused coupons for water rations from 1948.

જ

My father was 21 when he received his only professional degree, bookkeeper. Four years earlier, he had immigrated to Palestine, but due to circumstances he was never willing to discuss, he returned to his parents' home in Poland. In the photograph in the diploma, my father appears in a suit and tie, looking straight at the camera, a handsome young man, shy, yet proud. The left half of the diploma is in Polish, the right half in Hebrew:

My father had a strong, confident voice, masculine, but soothing. When, rarely, he would raise his voice, it would frighten those around him. At home, everything was conducted according to his wishes. At one time he must have been a real ladies' man. One of my aunts was secretly in love with him and, while I was growing up, sealed brown envelopes would still arrive at our house from a female admirer, a Dr. H. D., who apparently felt lost without him. During elections, he was the chairman of a polling station committee as the representative of the Mapai (the ruling party in Israel until 1977). On Memorial Day for Israel's fallen soldiers, for a few minutes he was part of the guard of honor made up of veterans of the Haganah (the pre-State paramilitary defense organization), which President Ben Zvi reviewed before the siren was sounded at ten o'clock. I was proud of my father, but also a bit embarrassed that he was not one of the fathers capable of standing stiffly at attention for a complete hour, next to the memorial flame.

With the establishment of the state, the word *buchalteria* was Hebraized to *hanhalat heshbonot* (bookkeeping), and my father became a government clerk. In time, he advanced, and almost made it to senior official. He was once photographed with the Minister of Transport at a ceremony inaugurating an airfield at the Dead Sea. On another occasion his name was cited in a news item in one of the daily newspapers. The article, which was cut out and kept in the bottom of the forbidden drawer, reported that one of the employees in his office had attacked him, and had been arrested and released on bail. No other details were provided.

I discerned my father's professional pride when I showed interest in the bookkeeping textbooks that rested in the bookcase, alongside the six volumes of the Mishnah (a codex of Jewish law), a Hebrew dictionary and a memorial booklet about the Jewish community of Bialystock. On the same shelves were summaries of lectures from the Economic History course that my father saved from his unsuccessful attempt to study economics at the university – the same texts the lecturer continued to read even when I arrived at the university. "A person needs a profession in life," my father told me many times when I was about to complete my military service and register for university. And he tried to convince me to study accounting, or at least economics.

When I was a boy, my father would take me on two buses to Mr. Gur Aryeh, the eternal secretary of the committee for "Workers Quarters B," a small neighborhood with narrow paths, flowers and a towering palm tree, located between the aristocratic Rehavia and Talbieh neighborhoods. Gur Aryeh's neighbours included a famous lawyer whose books are still cited, the father of an army Chief of Staff, an accountant, and a piano teacher who gave lessons only between 4 pm and 7 pm. Mr. Gur Aryeh, or "the nudnik" (nagger) as we referred to him in our family (because he would phone frequently, and ask, slowly and clearly, as if he did not expect us to understand, "is your father at home?") would open the door for us at five o'clock sharp. First, he would offer me a piece of bittersweet chocolate from a yellow box he kept in a drawer. Then he would sit me down in an armchair, and I would gaze at a drawing of David's Tower that hung on the wall, while my father discussed with him what to do about lost receipts. On the way back, between one bus and the next, we would stop at King George Street and my father would buy me a piece of peanut cake that had a whole peanut stuck in the center. Once a year we would ride to Mr. Gur Aryeh to pick up "the material." Then my father would sit during the evenings and do the bookkeeping for the committee. My father had wide ledgers with colored lines, lots of columns, and thirty rows corresponding to thirty apartments and tenants. From there, the numbers spilled over into two columns that had to balance before we could travel again to Mr. Gur Aryeh to return "the material" and receive the check that my father would endorse and pass on the next day to the grocer to cover part of the tab in his notebook.

When a new regulation was issued requiring that high government officers must be university graduates, my father was consigned to early retirement and became a teacher of bookkeeping in evening classes. The classes ran from 6:30 pm to 10 pm, with a break for *burekas* and Turkish coffee. He made his name as the author of the Exercise Primer in Bookkeeping Part 1. My father typed this slim book on a typewriter with a black ribbon that would get stuck whenever it was necessary to reverse direction. As a child, I used this typewriter to produce my street newspaper – a newspaper I founded, wrote, edited, and read, though not even a single edition was ever published. The bookkeeping primer bore my father's patronymic *nom de plume*, Ben Israel Meir, a reference to his father, a man who died with "Shema Yisrael" [the Jewish deathbed declaration of faith] on his lips and who left a slim booklet of polemical articles about the virtues of observing the Sabbath and the sins of our fellow Jews who went astray with communism, as well as sketches of figures from the halls of Torah study. Copies of the booklet will remain untouched in the National Library in Jerusalem and in a library in New York until the end of days, or until their pages disintegrate.

The exercises in my father's primer encompassed the entire theoretical world of Reuven, Shimon and Levy, the partners in "Furniture, Inc.," including movable property and cash, debtors and creditors, and a lot of doubtful debts. The transactions to be recorded were the sale on credit of six chairs to Mr. X and the payment of wages to the carpenter, Mr. Y. At the end of the exercise, the student had to deduct the annual depreciation on the company's typewriter and, if he did not make a mistake, he would find that the business had a small loss. To this day I do not know how the loss was covered. There was also a sample test at the end of the primer, with questions such as: "What is goodwill?" "What is the role of bookkeeping in a business?" and "Describe the duties of an accountant." The publisher was Moskowitz Book Publishers, Bat Yam. Moskowitz had a machine for duplicating stencils and some dealings with a bookbinder from Holon. My father orchestrated the marketing; every so often he would phone Moskowitz and ask him to send thirty copies via Egged Parcels for the evening course of the Workers Council in Hadera. The booklet had sequels: Exercise Primer in Bookkeeping Part 2 and Exercise Primer in Bookkeeping Part 3. I was filled with pride when I found my father's booklets at the university book store, among the books for students in the Accounting Department. When my father died, the books also disappeared from the evening courses of the workers' councils.

My father never spoke to me of his passion for women, or of his ambition to be a senior official, or even of his fears. I do not remember him ever saying "I love," "I want" or "I am afraid." But one night I saw my father as I had never seen him before.

The room was cluttered with household items: a bed, a bookcase and a radio that no longer worked, a dusty, empty fruit bowl, and lots of newspapers tossed on the floor alongside a pair of tattered slippers. On the dining room table, which also served as a work desk, there were plates with leftover food, left there since lunch. My mother was sprawled on the bed as always, surrounded by the stale stuffiness of unaired bedding. The broken wood shutters were closed and half-hidden by curtains that were once white lace and had since been refashioned by a decade of Jerusalem dust. My father sat in a brown dressing gown that was just about held closed with a threadbare cord. He sat with his back to the window, facing the bed where my mother was lying. I sat facing the window with my back to the bed.

My father made another attempt to balance the accounts of the committee of the Workers Quarters B neighborhood. The *nudnik* had already called five times to ask for "the material." My father would read a list of numbers to me and I would add them with the proficiency of a young student of mathematics. I was 21 years old. I was so bored. The totals swung between a deficit and a surplus and did not balance. I was impatient. I felt suffocated. I wanted to flee. My father said we had to start over again from the beginning. And again the numbers moved around in the shadows cast by the chandelier (two of its three bulbs were burnt out), and again he dictated the numbers and I added them up. And then my father clutched his balding head and said that if he did not manage to balance the numbers, he would have to kill himself.

❧

With a tone of seriousness befitting the occasion, I began my address to the members of the Senate with the following words: "I would like to express my strong objection to the plan to establish a program that focuses only on accounting." And I immediately continued: "Before explaining the reasons for my opposition, I would like to declare that I have a personal connection to the accounting profession. My late father's only training was in *buchalteria*. In my childhood, without a computer, I would spend many hours helping him to balance the books, adding debits and credits, and he would occasionally explain to me the rationale of the discipline he so wanted me to study."

I then proceeded in a serious, business-like tone:

Those who are admitted to the new program will undoubtedly be the cream of our youth. When they graduate, they will find work in the top accounting firms and will become part of Israel's elite, whose cultural make-up we are shaping, whether we like it or not. What will the members of this elite be like? They will be remarkably similar to, almost clones of, the images its critics portray. We are speaking of a talented and ambitious group of students who, at age 21, know what they are looking for in life. We will give them an entry ticket to the elite, extensive knowledge of accounting, and nothing else that this university could and should contribute to their education. Some might assert the cliché that accounting is an academic subject, but with all due respect to this new pillar of the scientific experience, I wonder how anyone can compare accounting to mathematics and biology and philosophy and linguistics. These are the subjects that we should be encouraging the outstanding students to study, rather than the elective course on "Accounting for Residents Committees".

At this point, the head of the Accounting Department interrupted me and shouted: "You don't know what you're talking about!" I hurried to conclude my remarks: "I ask each of you to use your independent judgment and answer the question of whether our curricula have true academic excellence as their objective, or whether our rhetoric is more *Pravda* than *Pravda*, and to vote accordingly."

I returned to my seat at the back of the hall and quickly buried my face in my father's *buchalteria* degree. No one looked at me except for one humanities professor who passed me a note saying that she disagreed with some of the things I said. Another professor, his hair parted on the side, wearing a sporty suit and black tie, rose to the podium and, speaking fluently, said that he was very surprised by my remarks. "We are not talking about *buchalteria* here," he explained, his face expressing distaste as he said the word, and went on to more or less say that I did not understand the difference between *buchalteria* and accounting: "Anyone can serve as a bookkeeper, but an accountant must have a BA degree. Accounting is an academic profession in every way, with international conferences and scientific journals…"

Then a vote was held and the program was approved by a large majority. A few people were actually influenced by my remarks and voted against it. Others only abstained, but no one bothered to count them.

During the following days, I was unable to forgive the head of the Accounting Department who had interrupted my remarks. I easily discovered that his comments were actually riddled with inaccuracies. I sent him and the rector a steady trickle of e-mail messages with evidence demonstrating that the approval of the program was based on erroneous information that he had presented. The embarrassed rector referred the program to some sort of committee and I said no more.

The image of my father that accompanies me now is his picture on the certificate from the Daughters of Zion: young, handsome, serious, shy and proud. I would run into that head of department on campus and was curious to ask him who his father was, but I did not dare to ask as I was afraid I would discover that he also had "a father". I do not know what happened to that program in the committee. Perhaps it was buried there. Perhaps it will reemerge and be unanimously approved by the Senate. Or, perhaps it was approved there long ago. I am no longer interested in it. All I really wanted was to complete the one balance sheet that my father and I did not manage to balance at the formica table in the middle of the room opposite the window, next to my mother's bed. After all, I just wanted to transfer one father from the liabilities side to the assets side.

Economics and me

This is how I usually begin lectures on economics and social issues:

> I would like to start with what I believe every academic should do when appearing in public, especially when speaking about political and controversial issues – to clarify the extent to which he is incorporating his professional knowledge in his remarks, whether he is expressing views with the authority supported by academic findings, and what part of his comments are nothing more than his personal thoughts and opinions. And so, I would like to declare unequivocally, without hesitation and even with a bit of pride, that my words here have absolutely nothing to do with my academic knowledge. Everything I say here is personal, based upon the entire range of my life experience, which also includes the fact that professionally I engage in economic theory. However, to the best of my understanding, economic theory has nothing to

say about the heart of the issue under discussion here. I am not sure that I know what an option is; I am not attempting to predict the rate of inflation tomorrow nor the productivity index in manufacturing the day after tomorrow. Of course, I am aware of the fact that you have invited me here to speak because I am a professor of economics who is supposed to know all this, and my ignorance definitely embarrasses me. So you ask why I have come here? Because as an economic theorist, I would like to state that economic theory is exploited in discussions about current economic issues, and I don't like it..., to put it mildly.

This statement is not just a pretense to exempt myself from a commitment to "scientific" criteria, and it is not intended simply to project an image that distinguishes me from other economists, or to boost my self-image. This introduction reflects what I truly believe. Nonetheless, it is clear to me that my remarks are received with skepticism. I myself would make fun of a professor of economics who begins a lecture by declaring that his remarks have nothing to do with economics, and speaks with an expression on his face that reflects his feeling of superiority over his colleagues and whose lecture could be seen as "spitting in the well from which he drinks." I am sure no one would invite me to speak about the government's economic policy if I were a professor of astronomy or an historian of the Middle Ages. Moreover, it is clear to me that my reservations do not prevent my listeners from continuing to treat me as a professor of economics (at most, an unusual one) and not just as a concerned citizen. And I suspect that despite my warning, there are those who regard my remarks as if they are spoken by someone with an authority whose existence I deny.

In this book too I make no claim to objectivity. I am not about to reveal to the reader some truth that I have discovered. On the contrary, everything I say here, even in an academic context (and I intentionally use the word "academic" since I do not think that the word "scientific" is appropriate for economics), is completely subjective, controversial and therefore perhaps describes me no less than it describes economic theory.

At the Hebrew University of Jerusalem, where I studied, I had the opportunity to listen to many distinguished professors. Two of them in particular contributed to the fact that I found myself engaging in economic theory. One is unknown in the world of economics, someone who is not slated to become an advisor to a Minister of Finance, and who has not even written articles on mathematical economics; he is the mathematical logician Saharon Shelah. When my friends and I emerged from the lecture halls on Mount Scopus and Givat Ram, our notebooks would be filled with the definitions and proofs we had gleaned meticulously from the blackboards that Shelah had filled and overfilled in courses on set theory and mathematical logic. When we understood what we had copied, we were astonished by its wholeness, level of conceptualization and logic. We encountered a strict and uncompromising insistence on norms of simplicity and precision. We were introduced to and learned to appreciate the beauty of a model, a statement and a proof. But the abstract mathematical concepts we learned in these courses (as in other courses in the Mathematics Department), actually appealed to us because of the interest it awakened in us in the world around us. We somehow felt intuitively that the formal concepts we were learning were directly relevant to real life. In our discussions over coffee in the cafeteria, we searched for the meaning of the mathematical statements not only as links between mathematical concepts, but also as statements about what intrigued us so much as young students: the interaction between people.

During my third year of study, I met the second teacher who is responsible for my academic pursuit, Menachem Yaari. As part of my work on a seminar paper, Yaari referred me to a wonderful book by Amartya Sen called *Collective Choice and Social Welfare*. This book has a very unusual structure. Each chapter has a parallel chapter with the same number but with an asterisk. In the chapter without an asterisk, a textual discussion is conducted about the various axioms of social choice theory, while in the chapter with the asterisk the textual discussion becomes a chain of precise definitions, arguments and proofs. When I read this book, I realized two things: First, that economics is interesting – a real revelation for me. And second, that the connection between our everyday world and the world of mathematical symbols is far deeper than I had thought previously during our coffee-bar debates. Before reading the book, I was like a child gazing at leaves, hills and shadows and imagining heroic figures in them, and feeling afraid of what I could see. After reading Sen's book, I realized that what we did in the cafeteria was actually an innocent foray into the core of economic theory. This is because economic theory is concerned precisely with the abstract concepts related to the interaction between people (the chapters without an asterisk). And the working tools of economic theory are mathematical models (the chapters with an asterisk).

Economic fables

Economic theory formulates thoughts via what we call "models." The word model sounds more scientific than the word fable or tale, but I think we are talking about the same thing.

The author of a tale seeks to impart a lesson about life to his readers. He does this by creating a story that hovers between fantasy and reality. It is possible to dismiss any tale on the grounds that it is unrealistic, or that it is too simplistic. But this is also its advantage. The fact that it hovers between fantasy and reality means that it can be free from irrelevant details and unnecessary diversions. This freedom can enable us to broaden our outlook, make us aware of a repressed emotion and help us learn a lesson from the story. We will take the tale's message with us when we return from the world of fantasy to the real world, and apply it judiciously when we encounter situations similar to those portrayed in the tale.

In economic theory, as in Harry Potter, the Emperor's New Clothes or the tales of King Solomon, we amuse ourselves in imaginary worlds. Economic theory spins tales and calls them models. An economic model is also somewhere between fantasy and reality. Models can be denounced for being simplistic and unrealistic, but modeling is essential because it is the only method we have of clarifying concepts, evaluating assumptions, verifying conclusions and acquiring insights that will serve us when we return from the model to real life.

In modern economics, the tales are expressed formally: words are represented by letters. Economic concepts are housed within mathematical structures.

A typical tale looks like this:

suit me well ? ' And then he turned again to the mirror, for he wanted it to appear as if he contemplated his adornment with great interest.

The chamberlains, who were to carry the train, stooped down with their hands towards the floor, just as if they were picking up the mantle ; then they pretended to be

holding something up in the air. They did not dare to let it be noticed that they saw nothing.

So the emperor went in procession under the rich canopy, and every one in the streets said, ' How incomparable are the emperor's new clothes ! what a train he has to his mantle ! how it fits him ! ' No one would let it be perceived that he could see nothing, for that would have shown that he was not fit for his office, or was very stupid. No clothes of the emperor's had ever had such a success as these.

And an economic model looks like this:

2 knows its actual value. In such a situation some new aspects appear. I will try to conclude from 2's behavior what the true bargaining cost is, and 2 may try to cheat 1 by leading him to believe that he, 2, is "stronger" than he actually is. In such a situation one can expect that the bargaining will continue for more than one period. I hope to deal with this situation in another paper.

2. THE BARGAINING MODEL

Two players, 1 and 2, are bargaining on the partition of a pie. The pie will be partitioned only after the players reach an agreement. Each player, in turn offers a partition and his opponent may agree to the offer "Y" or reject it "N". Acceptance of the offer ends the bargaining. After rejection, the rejecting player then has to make a counter offer and so on. There are no rules which bind the players to any previous offers they have made.

Formally, let $S = [0, 1]$. A partition of the pie is identified with a number s in the unit interval by interpreting s as the proportion of the pie that 1 receives. Let s_i be the portion of the pie that player i receives in the partition s: that is $s_1 = s$ and $s_2 = 1 - s$.

Let F be the set of all sequences of functions $f = \{f^t\}_{t=1}^{\infty}$, where $f^1 \in S$, for t odd $f^t: S^{t-1} \to S$, and for t even $f^t: S^t \to \{Y, N\}$. (S^t is the set of all sequences of length t of elements in S.) F is the set of all strategies of the player who starts the bargaining. Similarly let G be the set of all strategies of the player who in the first move has to respond to the other player's offer; that is, G is the set of all sequences of functions $g = \{g^t\}_{t=1}^{\infty}$ such that, for t odd $g^t: S^t \to \{Y, N\}$ and for t even $g^t: S^{t-1} \to S$.

The following concepts are easily defined rigorously. Let $\sigma(f, g)$ be the sequence of offers in which 1 starts the bargaining and adopts $f \in F$, and 2 adopts $g \in G$. Let $T(f, g)$ be the length of $\sigma(f, g)$ (may be ∞). Let $D(f, g)$ be the last element of $\sigma(f, g)$ (if there is such an element). $D(f, g)$ is called the *partition* induced by (f, g). The outcome function of the game is defined by

$$P(f, g) = \begin{cases} (D(f, g), T(f, g)), & T(f, g) < \infty, \\ (0, \infty), & T(f, g) = \infty. \end{cases}$$

Thus, the outcome (s, t) is interpreted as the reaching of agreement s in period t, and the symbol $(0, \infty)$ indicates a perpetual disagreement.

For the analysis of the game we will have to consider the case in which the order of bargaining is revised and player 2 is the first to move. In this case a strategy for player 2 is an element of F and a strategy for player 1 is an element of G. Let us define $\sigma(g, f)$, $T(g, f)$, $D(g, f)$ and $P(g, f)$ similarly to the above for the case where player 2 starts the bargaining and adopts $f \in F$ and player 1 adopts $g \in G$.

The last component of the model is the preference of the players on the set of outcomes. I assume that player i has a preference relation (complete, reflexive, and transitive) $\succsim_i$ on the set of $S \times N \cup \{(0, \infty)\}$, where N is the set of natural numbers.

The use of formal language has its advantages. Formal language imposes self-discipline on the storyteller. A teller of economic tales who uses formal language is obliged to spell out his assumptions precisely. When he uses expressions like "thus" or "therefore" or "it follows that...," he is exposed to objective criticism: the conclusion he draws from the assumptions must be formulated as a mathematical statement which must be accompanied by a proof.

A description of an economic model is like the introduction in a tale, presenting the heroes, their interests and the setting in which they operate. An array of rules by which the model is "allowed" to develop from its beginning to its end is called a **solution concept**.

Many solution concepts can be applied to the same model. We examine a solution concept according to the reasonableness of the assumptions it expresses, and we prefer solution concepts that can be applied to a large set of models. Formal language encourages the narrator to honor the requirement that the conclusion of the economic tale must be derived from the assumptions he formulated in describing the model and from the solution concept to which he is committed.

However, formal language also has its disadvantages. It creates the illusion of being scientific. Those unfamiliar with formal models tend to regard them as representing "absolute truth," though they are nothing more than tales. In addition, formal models narrow the target audience to those who were immersed in them. From my teaching experience I have learned that even the best economics students with the highest affinity for the subject have difficulty with the language of formal models, perhaps due to their persistent confusion between the formal model and its interpretation, and between the mathematical concepts and the words that accompany them. Moreover, when it comes to questions of economic policy, the model's formal mantle enables economists to create the false impression that their pronouncements are scientific and authoritative, and to conceal from the layman the assumptions the model uses. The barrier between the secret formal language and ordinary human speech almost completely prevents anyone who is not a member of the economic fraternity from criticizing "professional" economic claims.

Hotelling's tale of the main street

Harold Hotelling's model of the main street is a simple model that is considered to be among the more successful ones in economic theory. Two newsvendors compete for the custom of their city's newspaper readers located along the city's main street. Each vendor seeks to have the maximum number of customers buy the newspaper at his stand. In a simple version of the model, the freedom of action of each vendor is limited to choosing the location of his stand. The price of the newspaper is set by the publisher, so the vendors cannot compete against each other by lowering prices. Nor can they use violence to secure or enlarge their market share, and they do not have the legal right to appeal to the courts with claims such as "for generations, the whole street has been mine" or "it is only fair that I will control half of the street." As my teacher Menachem Yaari once noted, the economic agents in our models have desires but no rights.

At dawn, each vendor sets up his stand somewhere along the street. At lunchtime, each newspaper reader takes a break from his other pursuits and realizes that he cannot get through the day without reading the newspaper. The reader sees where the two newsvendors are located, and sets out to buy a newspaper from the closest one. (If the two stands are equidistant from the reader, the chances of the reader buying the newspaper at either stand are equal.) The diagram below illustrates the distribution of customers between the two vendors. The vertical line marks the center point between their locations. Everyone situated to the left of the vertical line buys from vendor 1, and everyone to the right of this line buys from vendor 2.

That was the introduction to the tale: we have described the characters participating in the situation and specified each one's range of choice and objectives. The conclusion of the tale is a description of the choices made by the two vendors. In other words, the two unknowns in the model are the locations of the two newsvendors.

We noted earlier that the principles by which the tale's conclusion is tested – that is, the solution of the two unknowns – can be found in the solution concept. The conventional solution concept for situations like the above is called a **Nash equilibrium**. This is discussed at length in Chapter 2. Here, I describe it in the context of Hotelling's model. The Nash equilibrium in this model must be a pair of locations, one location for each of the two vendors. In order to award this pair the title of "Nash equilibrium," the location of each vendor must be the best one for him given the location of the other one.

First, let us examine the situation in which both vendors are located in the center, the median point in the street with an equal number of buyers on each side. When one vendor is located in the center, the other will have less than half of the market share if he does not set up his stand in the center too. And if he does set up in the center, he will get half of the market share. Therefore, it is best for each one to set up his newsstand in the center when the other is located there. Consequently, a Nash equilibrium is achieved when both vendors set up their stands in the center.

Any other pair of locations is not a Nash equilibrium. If the two vendors set up in different spots, each can increase his market share if he moves closer to the other. Both setting up at the same location different from the centre point is also not an equilibrium: each one, by shifting toward the center, can increase his market share (and get more than half of the total, assuming that the other does not move.

We are thus left with a single equilibrium: the two vendors set up in the center. This situation, a single-equilibrium model, is ideal from the perspective of the narrator of the economic tale because the result of the equilibrium can then be regarded as the inevitable conclusion of the tale.

By the way, in this model, the competition leads to an outcome that is not ideal from the buyers' standpoint. If one of the vendors sets up at a location other than the center, none of the buyers will suffer and some will benefit, i.e., those who are now closer to the nearest one.

Hotelling's model has been applied to many situations. For example, instead of a main street of a city, economists apply the model to a situation in which two cola manufacturers must choose the sugar content in the product (and they cannot offer a range of products). The conclusion drawn from the model in this case is that both manufacturers should produce an identical product. Political scientists interpret each location point on the main street as a political position in a one-dimensional space (political right versus left, for example). Each candidate positions himself on the political map, aspiring to receive the maximum number of votes. Each citizen is situated somewhere in the political space and chooses the candidate closest to his own political views. Everyone agrees on the political geography and on the concept of distance in the political space. The model's single equilibrium is interpreted in this case as follows: if there are two parties operating in the political space, and if the subject of dispute is primarily one-dimensional, the platforms of the two parties will be identical, in the center of the political spectrum. Only a cynic would say that this conclusion matches the political reality in the real world. Even in the United States, the two political parties are far from identical. But Hotelling's model sheds light on the logic behind the efforts of the two parties, Democratic and Republican, to capture the center.

The tale of the three tailors

Imagine an island with six hundred residents, all dressed in identical clothes that require mending every month. Three tailors work at mending the clothes. For as long as anyone can remember, the residents of the island have been divided equally between the three tailors. Once a month, each resident goes to the same tailor whose services his father had used. Tradition, or decree, has set the price of the monthly repair at $5. Assume that the tailors have only minimal, negligible expenses. Each of the tailors would like to have as many customers as possible. However, even with great effort, none of them can do more than three hundred repairs a month. The residents feel that there is "hidden unemployment" in the tailoring sector. The tailors are often seen reading a newspaper, or dozing. It seems that two tailors would be enough and that it would be better if one of the tailors were to quit tailoring and find himself another job. In the language of economists, the situation is inefficient.

Let us say that all the tailors have various other employment options that influence their decision about whether to remain in the tailoring profession or to quit. Tailor A can expect to earn $900 a month in another profession, while Tailor B can expect to earn $600. Tailor C has limited alternative employment options and can earn only $300 outside the tailoring field. Each of the tailors will choose to abandon his sewing needles if his income from tailoring falls below his alternative income ("opportunity cost"). Currently, when the price of mending a piece of clothing is $5, it is not worthwhile for any of the tailors to leave this line of business because each tailor has two hundred customers and a monthly income of $1,000.

One day, the idea of the free market reaches the island. The traditions are shattered and the decrees canceled, and each tailor can decide on the price he charges for repairs. Each resident compares prices and turns to the tailor who offers his services at the lowest price. If more than one tailor offers the lowest price, the residents of the island will divide their custom equally between them. Each tailor attends a short course in modern business management and internalizes his role in the new economic regime: he must become familiar with the market and maximize his profits. What will happen on the island in the new situation?

The continuation of the Tale of the Three Tailors must provide answers to the following questions: Which tailors will remain in this occupation? What will be the terms of commerce between the tailors and their customers? As is customary in economics in this type of context, we will use a solution concept called **competitive equilibrium**. The concept of equilibrium imposes the following requirements for the rest of the story: (1) All customers will pay the same price for the repair of his clothes. (2) Each tailor knows the price of the service and compares the income he believes he can make in this work and his potential income outside this field. If the income in the other profession is higher, the tailor will leave the tailoring business. If the income outside of this field is lower, he will remain a tailor. (3) The number of customers the remaining tailors are interested in serving (supply) is equal to the number of islanders interested in this service (demand). Now, all six hundred islanders are interested in the service at any price. Since the tailors have no expenses, each one is interested in serving three hundred customers (the greatest number of repairs he is capable of doing a month). Thus, this condition demands that precisely two tailors remain in this business.

The logic underlying the concept of competitive equilibrium is that if the price of tailoring services is so high that the supply of tailoring services exceeds the demand, then the price will decline until one of the tailors closes his business. And if the price is low and the demand for tailoring services is greater than what the tailors are able to supply, the price will rise until another tailor returns to this sector.

We will now see that there is competitive equilibrium when the price of a repair is $2.50 (or any other price between $2 and $3), and only tailors B and C remain in this business sector. Each of the tailors (B and C) will have three hundred customers and each has an income of $750, which is more than either could receive in his alternative employment. Tailor A, meanwhile, earns $900 outside of the tailoring business. If he returns to this sector, he would earn $750 at most, less than what he is earning in another occupation.

In every competitive equilibrium, the price of the tailoring service will be lower than the price that prevailed in the old regime: If the price of the service were $5 (or higher), the tailor who quit the profession would figure that he could earn more as a tailor than he does in his new line of work. Only the two tailors whose alternative employment options are less profitable will remain in the tailoring sector; and the total output of the residents of the island will grow. An "invisible hand" generates the competitive equilibrium price and mobilizes the self-interest of the tailors and the islanders to correct the inefficiency created by the traditions and decrees that were recently canceled.

How does the market arrive at the competitive equilibrium price? The usual explanation offered in Introduction to Economics classes goes like this: The price of mending clothing prior to the cancellation of traditions and decrees was $5. After canceling the traditions and decrees, a price war erupts. One of the tailors who was "re-educated" concludes that it would be better for him to lower the price to $4.90 and thus create a situation in which all of the islanders would seek his services. Before long, the other tailors take note and also lower prices. And thus the price drops lower and lower until a certain stage when one of the tailors offers the service at a price less than $4.50. At this point, the tailor with the best employment alternative closes his tailoring business and engages in a different profession, and the island remains with only two active tailors.

Several assumptions in this story are not obvious. First, is it indeed so clear that the tailors will lower their prices after the cancellation of the traditions and decrees? We expect them to act only in pursuit of their own personal interests. But if a tailor is concerned only with his own earnings, it would actually be better for him not to lower the prices because he understands that any profit he would gain from increasing his clientele would be temporary and insignificant compared to the large loss he would incur in the future when the other tailors respond to this move and also lower their prices. The tailor would not need to speak with his colleagues in order to refrain from lowering prices. (Explicit collaboration between the tailors might be prohibited on the island under anti-trust legislation.) Stated simply, no tailor would want to start a price war.

Second, let's assume that the tailors are not so wise and fall into the trap the competitive atmosphere lays for them. Is it clear that the consumers will indeed choose the least expensive tailor? Until now, they have used the services of the same tailor their father and grandfather used. Now they need to compare prices frequently. If the price differentials between the tailors are not large, some customers will decide that the price savings are not worth the bother involved in comparing prices. Thus, a tailor may actually raise his price a little, relying on the fact that most of the customers will not bother to find another tailor offering the service at a lower price. If customers do not compare prices, the market might stabilize at a higher price than the competitive equilibrium price.

Finally, let us assume that all of the residents of the island regard the search for the least expensive tailor as a real national mission, an act that will serve the society as economists demand, and let us assume that the tailors are not so smart, and that price competition rages and leads to a drastic drop in prices, and that one of the tailors abandons the profession and finds alternative employment (and does not become jobless on the streets of the island), and that it enlarges the national pie. Then we come to the question: is this story as happy as it sounds?

The change generated by the competitive economic regime on the island did indeed lead to growth in the "national pie." However, the improvement also led to a change in the distribution of income. The situation is worse for the tailors and better for their customers. Is the income distribution better now? Are the tailors now receiving fairer compensation for their work? Is the price for mending clothes now more reasonable? There are no objective answers to these questions. Economics has no way of choosing between the new situation and the previous situation. The island's residents, all of them, are the ones who must make the choice.

The bargaining tale

A pie is to be divided between two diners; let's call them A and B. Both want as much of the pie as possible. Without an agreement on how to divide the pie, both will remain without anything. Both are hungry and want to eat their piece of pie as soon as possible. Unless they are willing to compromise, the allocation of the pie will be delayed, to the chagrin of both of them. The desire to receive as large a piece as possible leads to haggling; impatience leads the two sides to compromise.

A bargaining process is a procedure that enables the parties involved to reach an agreement. In the model of bargaining presented here, the negotiation takes places along a time axis. Each day, one side offers a proposal and the second responds, accepting it or rejecting it. Every time one side rejects the proposal submitted to him, he must submit a counter-offer, but not before the next day. In this way, the two sides to the negotiation exchange proposals until one of them accepts a proposal from the other and there is an agreement. At this point, the bargaining ends.

From the perspective of each of the two parties involved, each day that passes without an agreement is like losing a part of the pie. This loss might express the cost of time wasted in the bargaining process, or the mental effort involved in negotiating. Let us stipulate that from A's perspective, the loss incurred from each day of bargaining is equal to 2% of the pie. B is more impatient and from his perspective the loss from each day of bargaining is equal to 3% of the pie. Accordingly, if A has to choose between reaching an immediate agreement that would give him 57.5% of the pie and reaching an agreement the next day according to which he would get 60% of the pie, he would wait until the next day: The postponement would give him an additional 2.5% of the pie, more than offsetting the 2% loss he would suffer from prolonging the negotiation for one more day. On the other hand, if B has to choose between an immediate agreement that would give him 40% of the pie and an agreement for 42.5% to be signed the next day, he would choose to conclude the negotiation immediately: If he tarries, he will gain an additional 2.5% of the pie, which is less than the 3% loss he would incur, from his perspective, by prolonging the negotiation for one more day.

A solution, we said, is the principle that links the beginning of the tale to its conclusion. Here we will use the solution concept called **perfect equilibrium**. A perfect equilibrium is a pair of plans of action ("strategies"), one for each party to the negotiation, such that for each of the strategies the following holds: after each chain of events that might occur during the negotiation, the negotiator's strategy is the best one for him vis-à-vis the strategy of the other party. In particular, if a proposal is made that offers one side too little, a proposal that according to his strategy he should reject, then if the player who holds the strategy reconsiders his moves he would indeed choose to reject the proposal. In other words, if a bargainer's strategy includes a threat to reject low offers, then the threat must be credible.

One can show that the bargaining game could have only a single conclusion: the negotiation ends immediately. If A (the more patient bargainer) makes the first offer, he will receive the entire pie, and if B makes the first offer, A will receive 98% of the pie. The proof of this statement is not presented here, but the following section provides an illustration of the logic behind the result.

First, let us examine the following pair of strategies: each negotiator, when it is his turn to make a proposal, demands half of the pie for himself. And when his turn comes to respond to a proposal, he agrees only to a division that awards him at least half of the pie. In other words, each side always plans to offer an equal division of the pie and threatens to reject any proposal that gives him less than half of the pie. This pair of strategies is not a perfect equilibrium, because the threat to reject any proposal in which the bargainer would receive less than half of the pie is not always credible: sometimes it is not worthwhile for the negotiator to carry out the threat. For example, if A strays from his strategy and offers B only 49% of the pie, then B, according to the strategy, is supposed to reject the proposal. But if he carries out the threat and rejects the proposal, he expects – according to this pair of strategies – the next day, when he makes his counter-offer, he will end up with only 50% of the pie, assuming that A now keeps to his strategy. If B accepts A's proposal to give him 49% of the pie, he would lose 1% of the pie, but would avoid the loss incurred by prolonging the negotiation, which from his perspective is equivalent to losing 3% of the pie. Therefore, in this situation, B's threat to reject the proposal to receive only 49% of the pie is not credible, and it is best for him not to act in accordance with his strategy.

On the other hand, the following pair of strategies is a perfect equilibrium: A always demands 100% of the pie for himself and agrees to any proposal that awards him at least 98% of it. B demands 2% of the pie for himself and accepts any proposal, including one that gives him nothing. A's strategy includes a threat to reject any proposal that gives him less than 98%. This is a credible threat. If B offers A less than 98% of the pie, A will indeed reject the proposal, as his strategy suggests, as he expects to reach an agreement the next day to receive the entire pie, and the increase of more than 2% is larger than the 2% loss he expects to incur from an additional day of negotiation. B's strategy includes no threats at all because he plans to accept any offer.

This pair of strategies ceases to be a perfect equilibrium if we substitute the numbers appearing in the description of the strategies with other numbers. For example, let's examine the following pair of strategies: A always demands 60% of the pie for himself and agrees to any proposal that gives him at least 58% of it. B demands 42% of the pie for himself and accepts any proposal that awards him at least 40% of the pie. If A strays from his plan and offers B 39.5% of the pie, B would do well to accept the proposal. If he carries out the threat to reject the offer, he can expect to reach an agreement the next day that would give him 42% of the pie. The additional 2.5% would not compensate him for the "cost" (3%) of one more day of negotiation.

The model of negotiation described here, with the assumption that each player incurs a loss that is equivalent to a fixed share of the pie for each day that goes by without an agreement, "predicts" that the player whose time is less "expensive" will receive all (or nearly all) of the pie. The model perhaps clarifies the common intuition that a player whose time is more expensive is in a weaker negotiating position vis-à-vis a player whose time is less expensive. But the model does not describe reality, where things are always more complex, whether because the players' considerations are more complex and also include psychological considerations such as "if I already rejected an offer of 60%, I won't agree now to receive less," or because the negotiators do not always act in a rational way, or because negotiations in real life are conducted according to less rigid rules than this procedure of exchanging proposals.

I thought about this model just before completing my doctoral studies in Jerusalem. I was inspired by the market in the Old City in Jerusalem where I occasionally bargained when purchasing a Bedouin rug or Armenian plate. I really hate to bargain. Once, when I was fed up with the bargaining games in the market, I said to a trader, "Why don't we play a different game: you make an offer and I'll simply say 'yes' or 'no' ?" Ostensibly, I was trying to exploit my so-called professional expertise to design a different mechanism that would spare me the exhausting bargaining process. The trader smiled scornfully and threw out a price that I immediately rejected. But then the man provided me with an insight that put my dreams of using the bargaining model to reform the world into a proper perspective: "Tell me, did you think that I thought there was some offer I would make and that you would accept?" And then he added: "For generations, we have bargained in our way and you come and try to change it?" I parted from him shamefaced.

Tellers of tales

We have seen three examples of economic tales. Let's again ask ourselves the question: what is the connection between an economic model and reality? Different economists have different answers to this question. According to one view, an economic model is supposed to serve as a basis for making predictions about the real world, not the world of tales. Those holding this view perceive an economic model as an attempt to predict human behavior, based on data about the actions and interests of the economic units included in the model. According to this approach, a model is supposed to be an objective description of the real world, not a tale. The designer of the model would be happy to add more and more details to it to improve its ability to predict. If the model does not provide enough good predictions, it must be augmented with additional details. But the increased complexity of the model exacts a steep price: it is hard to understand and is difficult to solve.

According to another view, the objective of the economic model is to sharpen perception. A model is an intellectual exercise. Just as a soldier use simulations in training, the economist exercises his intuitions on a model before offering advice. The use of formal models helps to develop our intuitions about the way things occur in life. Thus, for example, economists who specialize in game theory have advised various governments to auction off public assets such as government companies and wavebands for huge sums. Others have been members of strategic teams hired by firms that participate in public auctions. These economists did not rely on a particular model, but claimed that their work with formal economic models sharpened their senses. I am not unequivocally opposed to this approach and I assume that those who claim that economic models have sharpened their perception are genuine in expressing what they feel. I also find myself from time to time looking at something from a perspective I have acquired from the study of economic theory. But I am quite sure that if instead of devoting my adult life to economic models I had engaged in a non-academic profession, I would view life from standpoints that are less abstract but no less useful.

Both of the approaches I have mentioned so far look for a purpose in an economic model. Students look for a purpose in the material they study, because "Otherwise, why study?" The research agencies and university presidents like to hear about purposefulness since it is easier for them to finance research that has a practical aspect. We economists are delighted when we find evidence of purposefulness in our work, because we are full of guilty feelings about devoting our lives to meaningless studies when the world faces innumerable problems.

I would like to advocate another approach, which does not aspire toward purposefulness and the practical use of a model. According to this approach, an economic model is not essentially different from a model in logic.

A model in logic is not a prediction of how humans judge whether a phrase in ordinary language is true or false. It is not a recommendation for a thinking person and it is not designed to educate people to think correctly. I contend that economics studies the logic of life, but does not engage in predictions or recommendations. We deal with the wide range of considerations that economic decision makers might take into account. We are satisfied even if the economic model is merely interesting. To be interesting it must focus on considerations that at least some people weigh before making a decision and taking action.

In particular, I do not think that the bargaining models that I myself have studied have significant predictive value; I am not more qualified than any reader (but also not less qualified than my colleagues) to give advice on how to conduct negotiations, and I do not feel that dealing with these models has sharpened my ability to understand the process of bargaining in the market. There are many models of negotiation and many solution concepts, and each combination of model and solution concept has its own internal logic. At most, we find links between natural ways of thinking and bargaining processes. That is all.

Yes, I admit that it is tempting for me to think of myself as a teller of tales, a philosopher, a researcher of the social sciences, in fact, anything but an economist. Whenever I am asked "What is your profession?" – for example, on the form for entering the U.S. – I do not answer "economist" but instead adopt the neutral title of lecturer. Besides the immigration official and the sleepy passenger in the seat next to me, no one will see the form, but I still always refrain from defining myself as an economist. I have limited knowledge of current economic issues. During most of my life, these issues have not interested me. I usually toss the economics section of the newspaper in the bin together with the sections on sports, fashion and health.

This book reflects my debate with myself about economic theory. On the one hand, I am captivated by the charm of formal models: tales emerge from the formal symbols, and these tales have almost miraculous powers over me. On the other hand, I am obsessively occupied with denying any interpretation contending that economic models produce conclusions of real value. I feel attracted to economics as a branch of philosophy and as an academic field in which an intelligent discussion of social arrangements is, or at least can be, conducted. But I also feel disgust for economics as an academic field that tends toward conservatism and helps the strong in society maintain their dominance, and thus serves people for whom I have little empathy.

Snow in Jerusalem

My perspective on economic models is completely subjective and describes me no less than it describes economic theory.

When I was a boy and winter came, I would peek in the morning from the window of my room at the two green trees outside and hope to see them white. I longed so much for snow that I wanted to be a meteorologist.

A meteorologist, I thought, is the first to know when it is going to snow. But several nights that started with a forecast of snow – "tonight snow will fall in the hilly areas" – left me bitterly disappointed in the morning. Then several mornings that dawned with an unheralded white vista led me to the conclusion that the meteorologist was not the first to know when it would snow. Instead, it was Aryeh Mansdorf, the neighborhood grocer – he was the first to wake up and say his morning prayers before setting out to arrange the bottles of milk.

Later, I wanted to be a lawyer who would defeat his adversaries in battles of intellect and razor-sharp logic. In order to prepare myself for this heroic task, I borrowed Samuel Hugo Bergman's book "Introduction to Logic" from the labor union library. This book did not make me a master of debate and did not equip me with a wealth of rhetorical tricks. The only thing I remember from it is the description of tin soldiers lining up in the courtyard. A resounding defeat in a classroom debate on "Youth Movements, For and Against" (I was "against") made it clear to me that personal charm is more helpful in winning an argument than understanding the law of syllogism.

I had the good fortune to grow up in one of the most wonderful areas of Jerusalem. Rabbi Meizel from the synagogue my father attended on holidays; the communist Sala Marcel, who made a point of eating pork just to annoy everyone; Aunt Hannah, who left her husband in Siberia and immigrated to Israel with her two children; the ritual slaughterer from the Yemenite courtyard; the widow whose son got caught up in crime; and the intellectual

Yaacovson, who wrote a book explaining the rationale of the Jewish commandments — all these characters instilled in me a sense of great awe for those people who understood the complexities of human interaction so well. As far as I'm concerned, the opinion of such people is just as authoritative for making social and economic decisions as the opinion of an expert using a model.

So, I do not know when it will snow and when prices will change. I am not an advocate of justice and have done nothing to change the social order. I do not feel entitled to advise anyone on the basis of my professional knowledge. I find myself denying that the models I work on can serve as a basis for predictions and, in general, I do not think that the appropriate test of economic models is whether they are useful.

If the models we develop in yellow notepads or on blackboards constitute a basis for predicting human behavior, it would be miraculous in my eyes. There are no miracles in economics, but there are wonders. In my studies in the Department of Mathematics in Jerusalem, I learned to see wonders in the world of formalities. I sometimes also see them in economic theory. I approach economics as someone with a sense of curiosity who is trying to understand the logic of human interaction a bit better. This may not be much, but perhaps it is not so little either.

1. Rational, Irrational

My father's rationality

I consider myself a very rational man, explaining all randomness with statistical tools and refusing to recognize the existence of the hand of fate and supernatural forces. I was born on Friday the 13th and scorn lucky numbers. I like Yeshayahu Leibowitz's rationalistic definition of belief in God as accepting the yoke of Torah and commandments. This definition freed me from feeling ashamed of my lack of belief in a God who showers me with mercy and is furious about my sins. I believe in making a calculated analysis of decision-making situations, and always consider it appropriate to ask myself what I can do, what my objective is and what action would be best in my pursuit of this objective. I am often unsuccessful in doing this, but I still continue to try. While I regard rationality as an ideal way of life, it plays an even more prominent role in my consciousness as a polar opposite to behavior that I do not respect: I feel revulsion toward astrologers, readers of coffee grounds, and all sorts of experts adorned with academic degrees, who manipulate their audiences emotionally and whom I suspect of being driven by self-interest.

I associate the rational approach with the path of study and learning. The opposite, irrational world is identified with urges and emotions. Rational versus irrational, mind versus emotion, study versus prayer – for me, all these terms describe the contrast between my father and my mother.

My mother was proud to be a scion of a family from the Slonimer Hasidic community, a small branch of Hasidism founded in the mid-nineteenth century that was nearly wiped out in the Holocaust. My father, on the other hand, came from a devout family of Mitnagdim (opponents of Hasidism). When my father wanted to berate my mother, he would accuse her of coming from a Hasidic family. Nonetheless, on the eve of Passover my father would send me to the son of the *rebbe* (the Hasidic rabbi) to get three *shmura matzos* (special unleavened bread eaten during Passover), and the *rebbe's* son would tell me that Eli, my mother's brother, had studied in *heder* (a traditional Jewish elementary school) with his father – none other than the great *rebbe* himself. The thought that my mother's brother had played as a child with the *rebbe* was for me like an encounter with royalty.

I hate situations of emotional frenzy. The only ecstatic experience in which I participated was when my father would take me to the Simhat Torah celebrations at the Slonimer Shtibel, a synagogue that appeared to have been copied from a faded photograph of a lost Jewish town and rebuilt on the edge of the field between the Beit Shmuel neighborhood of Jerusalem and the border. I was squeezed into a dense ring of men in their holiday *kapotes* (traditional Hasidic long black coats). The smell was at first like that of the bath house, until the scent of soap gave way to the stink of male sweat. The elders of the community would carry the smaller, lighter Torah scrolls, while younger honorees would be called upon to carry the heavy ones. The Torah bearers would be surrounded by young *yeshiva* students, who would cling to the inner circle. I, as an appendage to the outer circle, would bump into tables and benches stacked haphazardly at the sides of the room, grasping my father's hand on one side and the warm and moist hand of a stranger on the other side. I would try to move with the rhythm of the dance and mumble the words of the refrain that was repeated endlessly, despite the fact that I was unable to understand most of them. I still remember the words: "My God, my God, why hast thou forsaken me?"

But Simhat Torah was just once a year. During the rest of the days of the year, the Mitnagdim won.

My adolescent rebellion erupted when I was about fourteen: I wanted to become fervently religious and asked my father to buy me a *tallit katan* (Jewish undergarment with fringes). On an afternoon stroll, at the entrance to Mea She'arim, my father told me that he had no objection to the change, but that before I don the external trappings I should learn Talmud and study *halacha* (Jewish law). He even offered to find a suitable teacher for me. My father responded in a rational way by demanding that I "hear and understand" before "doing". He kept his cool and stamped out the rebellion without a battle.

My mother believed in every person's freedom of choice, even a child's, and her wish for me was that I would fulfill everything I felt good about, as long as it was not dangerous. My father, just like the rational man who stars in economics textbooks, always had a clear objective: ensuring survival – physical and economic. Therefore, my father supported every military action the government conducted, vetoed every request from my mother to take a loan in order to buy living room furniture, and scolded me about unnecessary expenses. That was why my father wanted me to be an accountant or economist.

The rational man

The rational man's pattern of thought constitutes the foundation for most economic models. At the beginning of each course I teach on microeconomics or game theory, I find myself conducting an induction ceremony into the world of economic theory in which I expose the students to the portrait of the rational man in economics. In order to endow this ceremony with the appropriate air of dignity, I tell them that I should launch the presentation with a presidential fanfare. And then I begin to recite:

> The rational man has preferences regarding the consequences that are likely to result from choosing various alternatives. When he is required to choose, he:
>
> 1. asks himself what alternatives he has;
> 2. clarifies to himself the consequence that would follow upon choosing each of the possible alternatives;
> 3. chooses the alternative that leads to the best consequence (as expressed in 2) in accordance with his preferences, from among all of the reasonable alternatives in the situation (as expressed in 1).

This is quite abstract and I will try to explain. In economics, models are nothing more than stories about interactions between units called **decision makers**. A decision maker in the model encounters decision problems to which he must respond. We have in mind situations like a buyer choosing a car from a catalogue. A fellow choosing a life insurance policy from among the plans offered in the insurance market. Parents deciding how many children they will have (a non-negative integer) by choosing at some point not to have any more. If I had to draw a decision maker, I would portray him as a person with two eyes, two ears, a nose and a mouth. He sits before a keyboard with many keys. His hand reaches out and must press one – and only one – of the keys. Pressing one of the keys leads to a particular consequence.

A decision problem is described in economic models as a set of alternatives available to the decision maker, who is required to choose exactly one of the alternatives in the set. In presenting the decision problem as a set of alternatives, it is assumed that the way in which the alternatives are presented to the decision maker does not affect his decision. This means, for example, that a default option – if one exists – does not influence the decision: the decision of someone who is deliberating whether to sign his consent to donate organs after his death is not influenced by whether the appropriate box on the form has a check mark that he can remove, or whether the box is empty and he can add a check mark to indicate his consent to donate organs. This also means that the decision maker's choice is the same regardless of whether the set of alternatives is described by a characteristic or explicitly. For example, the problem "Choose one of the four largest countries in the world" is supposed to be identical to the problem "Choose between the U.S., China, Canada and Russia." The order of presenting the alternatives is also not supposed to have an impact on the decision maker's choice: the choice between "yes" and "no" is not different from the choice between "no" and "yes."

All this is concealed in the innocent definition of the decision problem as a set of alternatives from which to choose. Of course, we are aware that factors such as a default option, the way a set of alternatives is described, and the order in which the alternatives enter the consciousness of the decision maker are indeed likely to have an influence on what most people choose in real life. However, we presume that **the rational man** does not take such non-essential factors into consideration and, therefore, these factors are excluded from the description of the decision problem. Thus, as if by the way, we insert elements of rationality into the description of the decision maker in economics.

In regard to the identity of the decision maker – we view a decision maker as an independent decision making unit whose choices are not influenced by other decision makers. We generally refer to a single individual, but sometimes a decision maker is a group of individuals such as a family, committee or commercial enterprise. On the other hand, there are cases when an individual, let's call him Moses, is split into two decision makers, Moses 1 is Moses after being slapped by his brother Aaron, and Moses 2 is the Moses who has calmed down the next morning. Moses 1 and Moses 2 have the same ID number and genetic makeup, but the considerations of Moses 1 and Moses 2 can be completely different, and neither Moses controls the actions of the other.

When we introduce a decision maker into an economic fable, we equip him with operating instructions that guide him in responding to all of the decision problems that are likely to arise during the tale. Thus, for example, the description of a young person who applies to a group of universities should include details about which university he would choose if accepted by more than one, i.e., his order of priority. If he applies to three universities – Jerusalem, Tel Aviv and Haifa – the descriptions should include what he would do if accepted by all three, if only accepted by Jerusalem and Tel Aviv, if only accepted by Tel Aviv and Haifa, or only by Jerusalem and Haifa. Another example: many economic models include a type of decision maker we call **a consumer**. We imagine the consumer receiving a monetary budget that he can use to purchase products that are of value to him. Each product has a price – the number of units of money he must allocate to acquire a unit of the product. The consumer must decide how to allocate the budget between the various products. A complete description of the consumer should explain what he would consume (that is, which combination of products) at *every* budget level and at *every* possible price structure.

It is possible to think of a decision maker as a machine that receives data about a set of alternatives he must choose from, and then creates output in the form of one of these alternatives. Psychologists and brain science researchers are interested in the structure of the machine that processes the data and reaches a decision. Traditionally, the economist is not interested, at least not as an economist, in the technical details of the machine's operation. He is interested only in the connection between the input and output, between the decision problem and the action chosen.

Here we reach the core of the assumption of rationality in economic models. A rational decision maker has a clear ranking of consequences in mind. We call this ranking **preferences**. When a rational decision maker faces a decision problem, he chooses the alternative that produces the best result in accordance with his preferences.

Let's take for example a decision maker who is entitled to a monetary reimbursement. The amount of the reimbursement is likely to depend on the date on which the decision maker collects what is owed to him. The result might take the form of "receives X dollars T days from now." Let's assume, for example, that the decision maker feels that postponing collection of the money is equivalent to a loss of $3 a day. Such a decision maker will prefer, for example, to receive $100 in another ten days (which is equivalent to receiving $70 immediately, from his perspective) rather than to receive $200 in another 45 days (which is equivalent to receiving $65 immediately, from his perspective). In general, he assesses the result "receives X dollars T days from now" by using the formula X-3T. This rule unequivocally defines the decision maker's preferences. The decision maker's objective function is expressed by X-3T. The choice of the best alternative means choosing the one for which the objective function gives the maximum value.

According to the assumption of rationality in economics, the decision maker is guided by his preferences. But the assumption does not impose a limitation on the reasonableness of preferences. The preferences can be even in direct contrast with what common sense might define as the decision maker's interests. According to this definition, a company director who chooses a strategy of production and marketing that minimizes the company's profits is rational. An employer who evaluates an employee according to the numerical value of the letters in his name (known in Hebrew as *gematria*) is rational. Someone who is concerned only with the welfare of someone else is rational, even if this concern is detrimental to his own existential interests. A person who does what he does because "they told me to do so" or because "it was the first thing that came to mind" or "it is not the best but it is nearly the best," or someone who tries very hard to do what is impossible, all are irrational according to the accepted meaning in economics.

It is not always clear whether a person is acting according to the paradigm of the rational man. When my daughter, Michal, was one year old, I wanted to check whether she displayed consistency in her choices. I knew that she distinguished between colors. We sprawled on the floor of the room. I placed three colored blocks in front of her – green, red and blue – and asked her to choose one of them. She took the green one. I rearranged the blocks in a different order and she chose the red one. Even after a dozen repetitions, no consistency was evident in her choices. I was really happy and so proud of her. Here was my daughter violating the most basic assumption of rationality – that there is some consistency in choices made. But then I realized that my excitement was premature. My daughter always chose the cube on the left. In other words, her choices were indeed consistent if seen from the perspective of the position of the cube rather than its color.

As if

According to the traditional approach, economists are not interested in the question of whether the decision maker's choice was preceded by a stage in which he actually conducted an explicit act of maximization, that is, if he chose the alternative that maximizes an objective function. The only thing that is important to the economist is that it is possible to describe the behavior of the decision maker *as if* he had conducted maximization. Let's look, for example, at the worker who wakes up after sleeping for S hours. Let's assume that the worker cannot control the number of hours of sleep but that he can decide how many of the remaining (24-S) hours in the day will be devoted to work and how many to leisure activity. Assume that in exchange for his labor, the worker will receive wages of W per hour. Let's assume that the worker always allocates half of his waking hours to work. That is, he works (24-S)/2 hours and devotes the same number of hours to leisure. The worker does not conduct any maximization, but acts according to a rule that is ingrained in him, perhaps without even being aware of its existence.

Ostensibly, it seems that the worker's behavior does not fit the model of the rational man in economics. Nonetheless, we will see that the worker's behavior can be described *as if* he has a particular objective function and always chooses the solution that maximizes it. The result for this worker is the combination of the number of hours of leisure (L) and the sum of money (M) he will earn that day. Let's assume that the worker's preferences among the group of outcomes are determined according to an odd criterion: the product of the leisure hours and the sum of money he earns. If he chooses L hours of leisure, he will work (24-S-L) hours and receive (24-S-L) × W units of money. Consequently, he chooses the number of leisure hours that will maximize the function L × (24-S-L) × W. In algebra class in high school, we learned that this function has a single maximum point at L = (24-S)/2. We found, therefore, that an employee who allots his time so that the function L x M receives the highest value possible will always (whatever S and W are) devote half of his waking hours to work. Maximizing this strange function is like describing the employee's behavior. I cannot imagine a reasonable person who consciously maximizes the product of leisure hours and the sum of wages. But for the economist, in order to qualify the decision maker as being rational, it is enough that he can describe his behavior *as if* he maximized some preferences.

I remember the moment as a student when I realized that the models in economic theory do not assume that the decision maker consciously tries to maximize his preferences, but only assume that the behavior of a decision maker can be described as if he had maximized some objective function. The words "as if" were magic for me then. Suddenly, economics appeared more abstract and sophisticated than I had thought previously. Years went by until I understood that there is also a potential for deception in this sophistication. On the one hand, decision makers' preferences in economics are presented only as a means to describe their behavior. In the previous paragraph we used the function of the product of wages and leisure hours only to describe the behavior of the worker who devotes half of his waking hours to work. Most economists, however, apply economic models to policy questions which require a criterion for the welfare of the individuals to be specified. Economists often identify an individual's level of happiness with the preferences that explain his behavior. By this approach, if the decision maker chooses alternative A when B is also possible, this means that indeed he prefers A to B. It is far from obvious that the preferences used to describe the decision maker's behavior correspond to his degree of happiness. Even if the decision maker's behavior can be described as the result of maximizing some objective function, the objective might not relate to promoting his happiness. For example, it is possible that he consistently works to achieve a "wrong" goal. And here is an absurd case: a decision maker has a clear concept of the essence of happiness, but he acts determinedly and consistently to actually diminish his happiness. A person like this is seen by economists as rational in the sense that he maximizes a clear goal – to worsen his situation as much as possible. But to identify his happiness with the preferences used to describe his behavior is like saying that the person is happier the less happy he is. This does not sound good.

In other words, "as if" is not only a magical phrase, as I felt back in the days when I was thrilled to discover the hidden treasures of economic theory. The underlying economic theory is not only that the decision maker can be described as someone who maximizes some objective, but also that he maximizes a function that expresses his happiness. It ultimately became clear to me that the phrase "as if" is a way to avoid taking responsibility for the strong assumptions upon which economic models are founded.

My entire professional life revolves around the definition of the rational man – someone who aspires to advance a well-defined objective or whose behavior can be expressed as the result of a process in which he asks himself what is desirable and what is possible, and chooses the best possible alternative. At the end of the induction ceremony that I conduct for my students I add some reservations about the status of the rational man in the real world. I emphasize that by using this definition we are not claiming that every person makes decisions in a way that is consistent with the definition of the rational man. I also note that the accepted definition in economics demands that the rational decision maker maximizes some function – but not necessarily his happiness. Yet it seems to me that these reservations fade away in the face of the magic of the clear formulation and joy of the formal description of the decision maker as someone who maximizes an explicit function. I believe that the image of the rational man that remains in the student's mind is that of someone who maximizes some function, and this function also quantifies his happiness.

Dependence on presentation

The professional literature is full of experiments that clash with the assumption of rationality. Psychologists, philosophers and economists conduct these experiments. Prominent among them are Amos Tversky and Daniel Kahneman and their followers. Those who worship economic thinking get angry. Those who do not like the "square" mindset of the rational man applaud.

Here is one well-known example (on the book's website, you can experiment with the situations discussed in this example, and the rest of the chapter: www.openbookpublishers.com/product.php/148). Physicians at the university hospital at Stanford were randomly divided into two groups. The physicians in one group were asked the following question (Question 1):

> An epidemic threatens the lives of 600 people. Two alternative and mutually exclusive plans of action are proposed:
>
> Under Plan A, 400 people will die.
>
> Under Plan B, there is a 1/3 chance that no one will die and a 2/3 chance that 600 people will die.
>
> You must choose one plan of action.
> Which would you choose?

The physicians in the second group were asked the following (Question 2):

> An epidemic threatens the lives of 600 people. Two alternative and mutually exclusive plans of action are proposed:
>
> Under Plan C, 200 people will be saved.
>
> Under Plan D, there is a 1/3 chance that 600 people will be saved and a 2/3 chance that no one will be saved.
>
> You must choose one plan of action.
> Which would you choose?

The need to choose between plans A and B poses a dilemma: Plan A is bad, because it will not prevent the certain death of 400 human beings. In Plan B, there is hope (a 1/3 chance) that the plan will succeed and no one will die; but there is also a significant risk that the number of dead will reach 600.

The choice between plans C and D also poses a dilemma: in Plan D, there is hope of saving all the patients, along with a significant risk that all 600 will die. Plan C is not especially encouraging, but it offers the certainty of saving a substantial number of patients.

Some readers will be surprised to discover that Plan A and Plan C are identical: the death of 400 people is equivalent in this story to saving 200 people. Plans B and D are also identical: 0 mortalities means 600 survivors, and 600 mortalities is equivalent to 0 survivors. The problem of choosing between A and B is the same as the problem of choosing between C and D. Therefore, a rational decision maker in the first group who chooses A would also choose

C if responding to Question 2; if he chooses B in Question 1, he would choose D in Question 2. The fact that A is identical to C and that B is identical to D is obvious once it is pointed out. But it turns out that there are many intelligent people who fail to note they are identical, even when they are asked to respond to the two questions one after the other.

In the original experiment, 78% of the physicians who were asked to choose between A and B chose Plan B, the alternative that involves risk. 72% of those who had to choose between C and D chose the sure plan, C. The physicians were divided into the two groups randomly. There is no reason to think that the hand of fate divided a large group of individuals into two groups in such a way that the characteristics of the physicians who responded to the first question differed significantly from the characteristics of those who responded to the second question. Thus, it is possible to conclude that about 78% of the physicians at Stanford would choose B if asked Question 1 and 28% would choose D if asked Question 2. The data do not rule out the possibility that 22% of the physicians would choose A and C, and that 28% of them would choose B and D. But, the data indicate that at least half of the physicians would choose B if asked to choose between A and B, and would choose C if asked to choose between C and D.

We have noted a lack of consistency among at least half of the physicians who participated in the experiment. In decision problems under conditions of uncertainty that entail losses, we exercise different considerations than in decision problems in conditions of uncertainty that involve gains. When we look at the decision problem from the perspective of loss, we are drawn to a plan that offers real hope of preventing the tragedy, even if it entails a risk of enlarging its dimensions if it occurs. When we examine the decision problem from the perspective of salvation, as a choice between two life-saving medical actions, we prefer to go for the sure thing rather than take a gamble that would enable us to save a larger number of patients but entails a significant risk that no one would be saved.

Kahneman and Tversky conducted this experiment using a routine experimental technique. As noted, the respondents were randomly divided into two groups, with one group assigned to respond to Question 1 and the other group assigned to respond to Question 2. This technique provides a solution for the concern that if the same person is asked to respond to both questions, one after the other, his response to the second question will be influenced by the fact that he had just answered the first question. It turns out that even when the same people are asked both questions one after the other, there is significant inconsistency between the answers to the two questions. More than 5,000 students of game theory were asked to respond to two questions posted on the web that are similar in format to the questions the reader can find on this book's Internet site. The students were asked the two questions in the order presented here, with a number of completely different questions inserted between the two questions. 72% of the students chose alternative B in the first question and far fewer, 49%, chose D in the second question. The result regarding the choice between A and B is very similar to those of the original experiment whereas in regard to the second question, the percentage of respondents who chose

D rose significantly, from 28% in the original experiment to 48% in the web-based experiment. Apparently, when the two questions were presented consecutively, some of the students did indeed become aware of the connection between the two questions and made sure to remain consistent with the choice they made on the first question. Nevertheless, more than a quarter of the students made the combination of choices B and C.

Begin and Rabin

1977 was one of the most memorable years of my life. I was in my first year as a doctoral student, full of enthusiasm about the world of formal models I had just discovered. In one of the classes, the lecturer referred to a simple model I had formulated and I was in seventh heaven. I had stepped out into the big world and was living away from my parents' home for the first time. We were a few serious youngsters who had founded the "Movement for a Different Zionism." We envisioned it as a harbinger of the formation of a large political group that would step into the breach against Gush Emunim, the Israeli settlers' movement. We were fearful of the messianism and extreme nationalism of certain national religious groups, and were disgusted with the settlement policy the Begin government was committed to and began to implement as soon as it took office. The excitement of political activity blended with the romantic intoxication of a Jerusalem summer and meetings that lasted into the small hours of the night in the quaint Nahlaot neighborhood.

I had already encountered Begin's rhetorical style when I was a child. My father took me to a soccer game only once, but many times to election rallies. At Menorah Square in Jerusalem and at the entrance to the Mea She'arim neighborhood, I heard Begin speak vehemently against the ruling Mapai semi-socialist party. My father would make fun of Begin, but still admired him enough to take me to shake his hand at a barmitzvah celebration where Begin was among the guests. When I was a child, I thought Begin's rhetoric made him look as if he were playing the fool or clowning. Fifteen years later, in 1977, I was amazed to watch him enthrall the masses. I felt helpless and frustrated by the reactions of many of my friends, who extolled Begin for his rhetorical prowess and in the same breath criticized the rhetorical poverty of our own forces. I, who believed in the power of level-headed argument, did not regard Begin as a role model.

Begin often explained his decisions in terms of carrying out duties and honoring rights: "We must all make an effort to... We have to... But we are also obliged..." He would start by saying "We must make sure that..." and ask "What should we have done?" In a meeting with President Carter on 19 July 1977, Begin reached new heights of rhetoric:

> Mr. President, in your country there are many cities with biblical names. You have eleven places with the name Hebron; five with the name Shiloh and seven with the name Bethlehem. Can you imagine a governor in one of these states prohibiting Jews from living in these cities? The Israeli government also cannot prohibit Jews from living in Hebron, Bethlehem or Beit El. It is our duty to...

Begin's arguments were generally based on "our rights" and "our duty." One could think that there is room for discussion and disagreement regarding rights and duties. Did our forefathers command us to settle in Beit El in 1977? Why are we bound by the wishes of our forefathers? Are there other obligatory commands that contradict this "duty"? However, in Begin's rhetorical realm, there was no room to examine the limits of the possible and to identify the desirable. The preferred status of an action derived from its being considered part of our rights and our duties and not from its being the best action in light of the limitations of the possible, according to our worldview.

Rabin, in contrast to Begin, had a measured tone and a matter of fact, down to earth style. I remember the satisfaction I felt one morning in the late 1970s when I heard Rabin interviewed on the radio. Speaking just like the rational man from the economic definition, he outlined the possible and the desirable, and after careful consideration, drew conclusions. During his victorious election campaign in 1992, Rabin made frequent use of the concept of priorities. In his book Service Notebook, he wrote: "I have no doubt that the dangers of peace are a thousand times preferable to the gloomy certainty of war." He asked himself what possibilities were available, even after he made a decision:

> I shall always remember the moment just after deciding to mount an action: the hush, the sound of the door closing; and then the silence in which I remain alone... In that moment of great tension just before the finger pulls the trigger, just before the fuse begins to burn; in the terrible quiet of that moment, there is still time to wonder, alone: Is it really imperative to act? Is there no other choice? No other way? (from Rabin's speech at the award ceremony of the Nobel Peace Prize in 1994).

The distinction between Begin and Rabin corresponded to the difference in style between the slogans of the right and those of the left in Israel at that time. The leading slogans of the right claimed rights ("The Land of Israel, all of it is ours"), made statements that were ostensibly factual ("The Golan is an inseparable part of the State of Israel"), and expressed prayers ("Messiah now"), while the slogans of the left quoted preferences ("Peace is preferable to the greater Land of Israel") and a demand ("Peace now"). It seems to me that the differences in style between the slogans of the left and right became less acute in later years, as all of Israeli politics was taken over by the culture of media advisors and public relations.

In the final analysis, did Rabin's preferences really have an advantage over Begin's rights? In my view, the answer is not unequivocal. Begin entangled Israel for generations with the settlement enterprise and embarked on the unnecessary Lebanon War, but also signed the historic peace treaty with Egypt. Rabin ordered the army to break the limbs of the demonstrators in the first intifada and was responsible as IDF chief of staff in the Six Day War for Israel's inhumane treatment of the remnants of the Egyptian Army in the Sinai, but his signing of the Oslo Accords ensured his place in history (and led to his death).

As years went by, I realized that I think more like Begin than Rabin in regard to the occupation and the occupied territories. My unconditional opposition to ruling over another people did not derive from my formulation of the objectives that the State of Israel is supposed to achieve or from asking myself which possible policy would generate the best result in terms of these objectives. I simply feel an absolute **duty** not to be on the side of the occupier and oppressor, even if the occupation is economically beneficial and brings peace closer. Nonetheless, I do not have a shred of sympathy for Begin. Even his signing of the peace treaty with Egypt and the fact that he was subject to periodic bouts of depression did not soften my anger over his demagogic antics. Like the times when I was a child and wanted to use a book of logic to prepare myself for asserting irrefutable arguments against evil, I still find myself looking for ways to understand rhetoric and long to defeat demagoguery.

Mental arithmetic

The following example is Kahneman and Tversky's. Students were divided into two groups. Students in one group were asked:

> Imagine that you have decided to see a show that costs $20. You purchased a ticket, but upon your arrival you discover that you have lost it. Will you purchase another ticket for the show?

The question for the students in the second group was:

> Imagine that you have decided to see a show that costs $20. Upon your arrival, you discover that you have lost a $20 bill. Will you purchase a ticket for the show?

Rational principles, it seems, dictate that the respondents should answer the two questions in the same way. That is, regardless of whether the decision maker lost a ticket or a $20 bill, he will have $40 less than he had before if he purchases a ticket and sees the show; and if he does not purchase another ticket he will find himself with $20 less than what he originally had and misses the show. Thus, whether the decision maker lost a ticket or a $20 bill, he faces identical problems of choice. Therefore, we can expect that a rational man would make the same decision in the two cases. But in the original study, only 46% of the participants said they would purchase a ticket after they lost a previous ticket, while 88% answered that they would purchase a ticket after losing a $20 bill. On my website, among 1,500 students who were randomly assigned to respond to one of the two questions, the results were less pronounced but similar to the original results: 64% and 80%, respectively. We can summarize: decision makers are more inclined to purchase a ticket after losing a $20 bill than after losing a previously purchased $20 ticket.

What is happening here? Decision makers assess the price of purchasing a ticket as the total expense involved in seeing the show. After losing a ticket, a decision maker tends to assess the price of an additional ticket at $40 rather than at its nominal value. After losing a $20 bill, he regards the loss as an event that is not directly connected to purchasing a ticket to the show, and he calculates the cost of the new ticket at only $20. This pattern of thinking is called mental accounting. The difference in the cost of a ticket, as it is calculated mentally, explains the readiness of some of the participants in the experiment to purchase a ticket in certain circumstances and not in others – those for whom the show is worth sacrificing $20 and but for whom a payment of $40 is already too much will purchase a ticket after losing a $20 bill, but not after losing a ticket.

Kahneman and Tversky also report that when the two questions were presented one after the other, the percentage of participants with inconsistent responses declined. The inclination of nearly all of the participants is not to purchase another ticket after losing the first ticket. But some feel embarrassed after becoming aware that they would have purchased a ticket after losing a $20 bill. A person's embarrassment in light of a certain choice reinforces the view that the choice is not rational.

My father died

After the army of physicians and interns and nurses finished treating my father, the physicians permitted me to enter the scrubbed and polished room, which showed no traces of the last battle. The room was lit by a pale fluorescent light typical of hospital evenings. My father lay unconscious on a wide bed, attached to tubes. The instruments rose and fell at the pace of an ebbing life. A physician told me that it was important that I hold his hand. I tried for a moment, but did not discern any reaction and let go. I sat near my father, I looked out from the hospital window on Mount Scopus at Jerusalem on Earth and thought about the nurse in the white robe with two open buttons who came every half hour to replace the cocktail of medications being pointlessly infused into my father's veins. Around midnight, I left and went home. I was awoken the next morning by a phone call informing me that the situation had deteriorated. When I entered the room, I saw only a white screen that hid the bed on which apparently my father's body was lying. The physician did not say a word. He assumed that I understood. He asked me if I wanted to approach the bed. Without hesitation I said no. My father was no longer there and as a rational man I found no reason to see the body of a dead person. And then the physician gently asked me whether I objected to having an autopsy performed.

I first encountered the concept of autopsies in posters by the Association for Defending the Dignity of the Dead, which often covered the walls of northern Jerusalem. The posters called on the public to fast and participate in demonstrations against autopsies performed by the "butchers" from Hadassah hospital. Sometimes the advertisements featured black and white photographs of a stomach or brain after the physicians had sawed, cut, emptied and sewn it. My father, despite his rejection of religion, still observed Jewish tradition to some extent. I do not know whether he feared God or felt nostalgic toward a lost world. I also do not know what he thought about autopsies, because we never dared to speak about death.

When the physician asked for my consent, I reminded myself that I was a rational man and that the operation would be performed on my father's corpse and not on my father himself. The lump of flesh laying there was at most a container in which my ex-father had resided. It was no longer my father whose body was to be dissected, and therefore why should I object to the advancement of science? If the dead were not operated on, the physicians would be less proficient and medical knowledge would be the poorer. If I did not consent to the autopsy, the responsibility for the death of future patients would also be on my conscience.

It was the dawn of the Friday before the Purim Festival. Mount Scopus was always the object of my dreams. I still sing to myself the ever popular hymn to Jerusalem "From on Mount Scopus" in times of stress. My sister was born on Mount Scopus during the pre-state era. My father worked there as a clerk during the British Mandate. We were cut off from Mount Scopus before I was born. Walking hand-in-hand with my mother on Ezra Street in the early evening, I would stare at the trees and gray buildings on Mount Scopus, which beckoned like an enchanted garden whose gate – the Mandelbaum Gate – was locked. I would sometimes watch Maman, the police officer, as he peered through his binoculars from the balcony on the third floor of the house across the street, anxiously tracking the twice-a-month convoy ascending the hill, until announcing that the convoy had passed. A feeling of relief would then sweep over the street. I did my first year of university studies on Mount Scopus. Later, my two children would be born in the same building in which my father died. Now, on that Friday before Purim, I thought about the limits of rationality.

The physician explained to me that by law I could not sign the forms for an autopsy on the spot, and needed to wait six hours after being notified of the death before signing the authorization. I was impressed by the logic and humaneness in the law. But it was impossible to tarry. The autopsy needed to be completed before the start of the Jewish Sabbath on Friday evening, and Friday was a short day. I controlled myself and did not expose my emotions. I just asked the physician, with the fear that characteristically accompanies questions posed to physicians, whether it was probable that someone's life would be saved as a result of the post mortem. Without hesitation he answered in the affirmative. He explained that an autopsy would help physicians and students understand my father's heart illness and that this might help in treating similar patients in the future. The physician had a pleasant countenance and wore a *yarmulke* (skull cap). At that moment, the *yarmulke* was for me a guarantee of his honesty.

Six hours later, I hurried back to the hospital to sign the required form. Before I signed, I stipulated that the post mortem should only involve the parts of his body affected by the disease. The physician expressed satisfaction with my response and promised that my request would be honored.

On Sunday afternoon, a few of my father's acquaintances and some friends gathered at the funeral home in the Sanhedria neighborhood. The burial society in Jerusalem had a bad reputation at the time, but I was impressed by the respect and sensitivity the thick-bearded undertakers showed to the mourners. As is customary, I was asked to accompany the undertakers to identify the corpse, which had been cleansed, wrapped in a shroud and prepared for burial. One of the undertakers asked me in a despondent tone whether I had consented to an autopsy. I nodded hesitantly, like someone who was caught red-handed. I stuttered that I had authorized operating only on the parts of the body related to my father's illness. The undertakers glanced at me with skepticism. Slowly, they unwrapped the bandages from the skull. It was the first time in my life that I looked upon the face of a dead person. My father, with his large face and without his false teeth, had already looked shrunken when he was in the hospital. I saw now that the skull had been cut open and sewn, as if they had emptied it. Then the undertaker covered the head again with the shroud.

Apparently, I had allowed myself to be deceived. Later, I also failed to fulfill my father's last wish – that I recite *kaddish*, the mourners' prayer, during the *shiva*, the week-long period of mourning. I went to the synagogue once for *mincha*, the afternoon prayer service, but I felt out of place there and did not go back again. My father was dead, and a rational man has no reason to honor the wishes of dead people. Nonetheless, why did it bother me that my father's brain had been cut? And why will I not forgive the physician who did not keep his word? And why did I not fulfill my father's last wish? And why does this bother me at all?

Looking for reasons

Tversky and Simonson asked the individuals in one group to choose between two alternatives: $6 in cash or a high-quality pen. Some 36% of them chose the pen. The individuals in the second group were asked to choose between three alternatives: $6 in cash, the same high-quality pen or a simple pen that was obviously inferior to the high-quality one. The percentage of those who chose the high-quality pen **rose** to 46%.

What is the explanation for this finding? Some of the individuals presumably have no interest in a pen and they would choose $6 when responding to either of the two questions. Some of the individuals may actually need a pen and in any case would choose the high-quality pen. But there are some individuals for whom the choice between the high-quality pen and the cash is not clear-cut. The existence of an additional alternative, a simple pen, provides "a good reason" to resolve this indecision and to choose the high-quality pen: the high-quality pen is clearly preferable to the simple pen, while the $6 is not obviously preferable to the simple pen.

On this book's website I cannot give out pens (and do not wish to do so). Therefore, two similar, but hypothetical, questions are posed on the site. Half of the readers are asked to respond to the following question:

> Assume that you are planning a trip and are interested in buying a digital camera. You find a store that sells three models produced by the same manufacturer. The models and their prices are quite similar to one another. The only differences between them is the score they received in a professional magazine and the number of pixels.
>
> Model A received a score of 9.1 and has 6 megapixels.
> Model B received a score of 8.3 and has 8 megapixels.
> Model C received a score of 8.1 and has 7 megapixels.
>
> Which model would you choose?

The other readers are asked to respond to an identical question – except for the fact that they must choose only between models A and B.

More than 1,500 students were asked to respond to one of the two questions prior to the publication of the book and the following results were received: among those who had to choose between models A, B and C, 65% chose

B and only 1% chose C. These results show the alertness of the participants in the experiment, even without offering real prizes. Among those who had to choose between A and B only, the percentage choosing B declined to 53%.

In this experiment, we compared the choices of decision makers who chose between A and B with those who chose between A, B and C. It turns out that the percentage of individuals who chose B from A, B and C was significantly higher than the percentage who chose B from only A and B. The decision makers who would choose B if choosing from the larger selection and A if asked to choose from the smaller selection cannot be described as rational: if a rational decision maker has preferences and B is the preferred alternative from among A, B and C, then B should also be the preferred alternative between A and B.

Here is another, similar example, this time from Shafir, Simonson and Tversky: individuals in one group had to choose, hypothetically of course, between A, a camera priced at $170, and B, a more sophisticated camera priced at $240. A low percentage of individuals in this first group chose B. The individuals in another group were given a third possibility, C, a much more sophisticated camera, priced at $470. And here, with the addition of the very expensive camera, the percentage of those choosing B rose (to some extent). A reasonable explanation for the change is that adding the expensive camera C made B into the middle option between A and C. When we arrange the alternatives in our minds linearly, the central location of an alternative is a reason to choose it.

Was it necessary to conduct experiments to prove the tendency of people to choose the middle option? This is well known not only to those engaged in marketing but also to my son, Yuval. When he was small, he told me that when his favorite fast food chain added an extra-large cup to the drinks menu, in addition to the large and medium cups, it was conducting a marketing ploy aimed at encouraging people to choose the large cup. This logic should have also led to the conclusion that in an election battle between a candidate from the right and a candidate from the left, it would be beneficial for the former if an extreme right-winger joins the race. Political experience shows that this is not always true: adding an extreme right-wing candidate often arouses aversion toward the moderate right-winger.

No one argues that the irrational considerations attributed here to decision makers are always decisive considerations. All of the examples presented here are only intended to illustrate the existence of considerations that sometimes influence decision makers and are contrary to the assumption of rationality. We have a lot to learn before understanding when these considerations arise in decision making and what determines their weight vis-à-vis other considerations.

What would my mother have said?

We use expressions like a dead person rolling over in his grave, my grandmother would have been happy to see me now, or, I observe the Sabbath because my forefathers observed the Sabbath. In our dreams, we see our deceased loved ones summoning us to do things that we might not have done if they had not appeared to us. For those who believe that the deceased are situated somewhere and are watching over us until we are gathered up to join them, it is easier to justify such behavior as rational. But as someone who believes that the souls or spirits of the dead are not hovering anywhere, I do not have much respect for those who use the kingdom of the dead to try to influence what happens on the planet of the living.

On one Rosh Hashanah (Jewish New Year) morning in faraway Princeton, I was informed that my sister had been rushed to a hospital in Jerusalem. At the end of the holiday, en route to Israel, I prepared myself for the worst. At the entrance to the hospital ward, a physician met me and explained her condition in detail: a "manufacturing defect" of nature had been discovered in one wall of an artery in the brain; nature had been negligent and had not provided a warranty. The wall of the artery was too thin and, with age, could not withstand the pressure. It had inflated like a balloon and exploded; its contents had leaked and perhaps caused damage to adjacent brain cells. There was a probability of 90%, the physician said, that the initial leak would lead to a second and fatal leak. The solution: a dangerous operation – though its description sounded like a routine plumbing operation. And here the physician confronted me with the most difficult decision of my life: the operation could be performed in Jerusalem, where the surgeons had limited experience with this procedure, or we could fly my sister to a medical center in the U.S., with the most experienced physicians in this type of surgery. On the one hand, undergoing the operation in the U.S. would diminish the risk of irreversible damage that could occur during surgery. On the other hand, it would involve a logistical project the like of which I had never had to contend with in the past. I was concerned about detaching her from the supportive environment. I also felt a twinge of fear about the possibility that in a foreign environment she might ultimately be operated on by a surgeon who did not have extensive experience. It was impossible to receive an unequivocal recommendation from the physicians. This situation arose soon after the community of neurosurgeons in Israel had been harshly attacked by a public figure who had traveled overseas for a brain operation and complained about the ostensibly inferior professional capabilities of neurosurgeons in Israel. The physicians were on the defensive and showed a lack of confidence in their recommendations. Friends I visited at 2am offered me conflicting advice.

Only rarely had I faced a real dilemma that was so similar to the decision problems under uncertainty that we discuss in our models. The alternatives were clear: an operation in Israel, or an operation in the U.S., or no operation. The last option was clearly inferior to the other two. The results were a matter of chance and the dice were in the hands of God. I had time to consult, learn and weigh the arguments. It was solely my decision to make. I was an adult and had even written several papers on the theory of decision making. If decision making theory has any practical value, it should have become evident then.

I lay on my bed and felt a tightness in my chest, signs of the tension and distress I was experiencing. I could not decide. I needed a convincing reason. And then I found it. "What would my mother have said if she were alive?" I asked myself, despite the fact that my mother had died several months earlier and even before her death had lost the ability to make real decisions. "My sister belongs to our mother. Our mother is responsible for my sister's fate and she will decide." Everything became clear and the dilemma was resolved: it was clear that my mother would have chosen for my sister to be operated on in the place where she was born and in the city in which she lived. The decision was made.

They do not understand the causal connection

Let's return to the picture of the decision maker who sits at the keyboard and knows that each keystroke leads to a given result. Let's say that we know and that he knows that pressing the A key leads to receiving $1 and pressing the B key leads to receiving $2. It is clear to us that the decision maker is interested in receiving as much money as possible: he says so, and every time that we offer the decision maker two envelopes with $1 and $2 he chooses the larger sum. Rationality, as we understand it in life and also as it is perceived in economics, requires that the decision maker understands the connection between pressing the A or the B key and the consequences ($1 or $2, respectively) and that he will press the B key. We can state this in a more abstract way: when there is a causal connection between an action and a result, the assumption of rationality includes the requirement that the decision maker is aware of the causal connections and will choose the action that will generate the preferred result, without making an error.

But human beings err, and do so systematically. Here is another example by Tversky and Kahneman:

Imagine a die with six sides, four of them green (G) and two of them red (R).

You must choose one of three strings of the letters G and R. The die will be rolled 20 times and you will receive $25 if the series of results includes the string you chose.

The three strings are:

1. RGRRR
2. GRGRRR
3. GRRRRR

Which string would you choose?

Choosing any of the three strings will lead to a result that in our professional terminology is called a **lottery**. If the string appears in the series of rolls of the die, the decision maker will receive a prize; if the string does not appear, he will not receive anything. It is reasonable to assume that the decision maker will prefer one lottery over another if it offers him a higher probability of winning a prize.

We note that every series that includes the second string (GRGRRR) also includes the first string (RGRRR). Every series of rolls of the die that awards a prize to someone who chooses the second string will also award a prize to those who choose the first string. Moreover, the string RRGRRR is the first string with the addition of another R at the beginning; thus, there are series that award a prize to those who choose the first string but not to those who choose the second string. Therefore, without calculating probabilities, one can discern that the first alternative offers a higher probability of winning a prize than the second alternative. Nonetheless, the overwhelming majority (65%) of the 125 students who participated in the original study chose the second string (GRGRRR). A similar result was found among 2,000 students who responded to the question (without receiving any real reward) as presented on the book's website: 59% chose the second string. And, incidentally, only 4% chose the third string (GRRRRR), which is easily seen to be less likely than the second string.

As noted, the rational decision maker must be aware of the causal connections between his choice and the result that derives from it, and he is supposed to choose an action that generates the result that he views as preferable. This assumption is sometimes violated due to errors, as in the experiment discussed here. It is clear that most of the respondents misunderstood the connection between the choice of the string and the probability of winning the prize. They did not understand that choosing the string GRGRRR means choosing an option with a lower probability of winning than the string RGRRR. The reason, apparently, is related to the fact that probability is often confused with representativeness. Given that the probability of the result G on any roll of the die is 2/3, the string RGRRR, in which only 1/5 of the letters are G, is perceived as less typical than the string GRGRRR, in which 1/3 of the letters are G. But, the probability of finding the string RGRRR in the series of rolls of the die is always greater than the probability of finding the string GRGRRR.

Not only errors hinder the understanding of the connection between a choice and its result. Sometimes the problem stems from the fact that we feel that we are able to influence the connection between the action and result, despite knowing full well that we have no such influence.

Imagine that you are a student. The teacher, who generally means what he says, announces that a memorization test will be held the next day on a text you have never read, and you would like to achieve a high score. You have to decide whether or not to prepare for the test. If you prepare, you will have to give up your favorite leisure activity, but you will ensure your success in the test. If you do not prepare, you will be able to spend your time as you wish, but you will fail the test. You clearly understand the connection between the action and the consequence. As a rational person, you will weigh the fun you are missing while preparing for the test and the satisfaction of success, on the one hand, against the pleasure derived from your leisure activity and the unpleasantness of failing the test, on the other. But let's assume that you noticed that in the past a strange coincidence has occurred: when you repeated a secret word, the test did not take place. If you choose to use your magical power and do not prepare for the test, you will fit the definition of being irrational despite the fact that you are doing your best within the framework of your beliefs and are trying to affect the connection between an action and its result. It will immediately become clear that you would not be the only one I would label as irrational...

Whisper

In high school, I was a good student, but only in the subjects that interested me: mathematics, Jewish law and citizenship. I did not do homework in the rest of the subjects. I would come to class before everyone, lie in wait for the first students and copy from them the homework in all the subjects I detested – literature, history, chemistry and biology – in return for the homework I prepared in math. The school conducted many surprise exams. The teacher would enter the classroom and pronounce the words that even now unnerve me a bit: "Take out paper for a test." I usually did not know the answers to the questions in the test and I became expert in copying them from my neighbor behind the broad back of my friend Yuval, who sat in front of me. During the moments of dread, when the teacher entered the classroom, I discovered a surprising correlation. Always, yes always, if I muttered the words "There is going to be an exam, there is going to be an exam" when the teacher was about to enter the classroom, there wouldn't be one. All of the exams took place on days when I failed to mutter my abracadabra.

This is how I encountered the power I have over the events in the world. When I say to myself: "This bad thing will happen," it actually does not occur. Just yesterday I lost my university ID card. The loss ignited an exaggerated burst of emotions in me. The ID card can be reissued. In the worst case, I would need to inquire about the procedures for replacing a lost ID card, to report the loss, to call and check the office hours, to stand in line until the new ID is issued… that's all. Really not so terrible. Nonetheless, I was terribly agitated. I looked in my wallet again and again; I searched everywhere and did not find it. I returned home to check whether the ID had perhaps fallen from my pocket when I was undressing or dressing. Nothing. It was not on the floor, not on the bed, and not under the bed. There was no ID card anywhere. I decided to check just one more time in case it was hiding in my wallet after all. But before I began the final probe, I muttered to myself: "The ID card is lost, the ID card is lost." I again rummaged through the wallet and… there it was, in one of the pockets of the wallet, tucked behind a credit card.

I did not pray to God. I did not speak with creatures from outer space. All I did was note the connection between what I say and what happens, a dependence that has proven itself time and again as an act of magic. As a rational person, I am struck by the urge to look for an explanation for this strange coincidence. Of course, I suspect that the success of my spell is related to the fact that I chose to use it in cases when it was likely that the thing I feared would not really occur in any case. The rational person within me protests: why should I shatter this wonder? After all, I had found an effective tool for protecting myself in stressful situations. And perhaps I had simply reached the limits of my own rationality.

Experiments

The heroes of most economic models are rational decision makers. The traditional economic view, the one that dominates in the textbooks at least, asserts that the assumption of decision makers' rationality enables us to describe human behavior quite accurately. The flood of experimental results in the field of economics, primarily from cognitive psychology, contradicts this view.

Results that are inconsistent with the model of the rational person elicit skeptical reactions (sometimes justifiably). The attitude of economists toward results that conflict with the paradigm of the rational man reminds me of the natural reaction to the optical illusion generated when subconscious mechanisms create a picture that does not conform to our perception of the world. In both cases, we smile, become irritated, suspect that someone is pulling a fast one on us, are happy to discover that even "perfect" beings fall into the snares that nature sets for us all, and we look for explanations.

Some criticize the experiments pertaining to decision making because the participants are offered insignificant incentives. The important decisions of life, the critics say, involve interests that are much more significant than a few dollars and therefore we cannot infer what people will do when faced with major economic decisions from the way they behave when offered the chance to earn negligible sums. I do not agree with this criticism. First, not only fateful decisions are important. In life, people make many small decisions and the cumulative economic impact of these decisions is significant. And second, most of the major economic decisions are made by people for whom such decisions are an everyday matter. The small decisions we make in life are no less important to us than the major decisions of the rich and powerful are to them. I see no reason to think that when senior executives decide on matters involving millions they exercise different considerations than those that common folks use when making decisions about a few dollars.

In most of the experiments we mentioned in the previous sections, the participants were only asked to imagine a decision problem and did not receive any compensation (not even symbolic) related to their choices. In my view, material compensation for participants in experiments is completely unnecessary. People are very good at imagining hypothetical situations. The fact that the results of the experiments in which no material incentives were provided are very similar to those received when participants were given material incentives indicates that offering incentives usually makes no real contribution to the identification of patterns of thinking used in decision making.

It is customary to evaluate research results via a statistical test. At best, this entails an attempt to assess the chance that we are drawing an erroneous conclusion from the data. For example, let's return to the question of the epidemic that was presented to physicians at Stanford. In the original experiment, of 152 physicians who responded to Question 1, 109 (78%) chose option A. Of 155 physicians who responded to the same but differently worded question, Question 2, only 34 (28%) chose C. We deduced from these results that the differences in wording between the two questions influenced the responses. We only assigned the title rational to those who chose A in the first question and C in the second, or B in the first question and D in the second. We concluded that a large group of individuals acted irrationally. But perhaps this conclusion is wrong and the differences in percentages between those who chose A in the first question and C in the second question can be attributed to pure coincidence? Perhaps all of the physicians at Stanford are rational, but some prefer the sure plan (A or C) while others prefer the more risky plan (B or D)? Perhaps, by sheer coincidence, the physicians were divided into the two groups in such a way that it just happened that more of those who preferred A (and, therefore, also C) were in the group asked Question 1, while more of those who preferred B (and, therefore, also D) were in the group asked Question 2?

A statistical test is designed to examine the extent of unreasonableness of the assumption that the results we received were only coincidental. We assume that all 307 participants are rational and would respond in the same way to the two questions: 143 of them prefer A to B (and, therefore, also C to D), while the other 164 participants prefer B to A (and, therefore, also D to C). A statistical test is based on assumptions about the random factors involved. The test we employ here (Fisher's exact probability test) assumes that the 307 participants were randomly assigned to two groups, one with 152 participants who responded to Question 1 and the second with 155 participants who responded to Question 2. The test assumes that all of the possible distributions of the 307 participants into two groups of 152 and 155 have the same probability. The test calculates the probability that the randomness created a distribution that is so biased that at least 109 of those who preferred A (and C) happened to be in the first group. Statistical programs greatly facilitate such calculations and it turns out that the probability of such an event is very (very!) close to zero. It is so close to zero that the possibility that the results are consistent with the hypothesis of rationality is unreasonable, and we reject the hypothesis. Incidentally, it was not necessary to have such dramatic results in order to reject the hypothesis. According to the conventional criteria, the test results would be considered significant even if the percentage of those choosing C dropped from 78% to just 72% (and not to 28% as occurred).

I have not addressed statistical tests at all in this chapter. The findings are so clear that it seems to me that such an addition would constitute nothing more than paying lip service to the professional conservatism expected in such reports. Incidentally, Kahneman and Tversky, for example, also did not bother to conduct (or at least to report) a statistical test that examined the results they obtained in the epidemic problem.

In general, the mechanical use of the concept of statistical significance is dangerous. The logic in its use rests upon important assumptions that are usually ignored or taken for granted but which should be examined. Researchers and newspaper readers love to use indices and rarely ask themselves what stands behind them. For example, the conventional tests of significance in economics completely ignore factors such as errors in measurement, documentation, analysis and reporting – factors that could have a major impact on the validity of the results. And, of course, the researchers have interests and biases and these, consciously or subconsciously, are liable to influence the reported results. It seems to me that the uncertainty regarding the credibility of the researchers is much more significant that the uncertainty taken into account in the conventional statistical tests. Therefore, I would be more impressed by two experiments conducted by two different researchers with small samples and results that are not considered significant, than an experiment conducted by one researcher with a sample twice as large and a result that is considered significant.

Is there any need for experiments at all?

Experiments are born in the feverish and fruitful mind of a researcher who is not detached from reality and knows how to surmise the considerations that pass through the minds of human beings faced with decision making problems. Whoever conceived the problem of the lost theater ticket certainly knew that people feel compelled not to purchase another ticket after losing the original one because the loss makes the purchase seem more expensive. The researcher understood that some of the participants find this consideration to be decisive when deliberating whether to purchase another ticket, while some take comfort in thinking that it really does not cost $40, but just $20. The product of the experiment is qualitative, supporting the assumption that more people would include the loss in their calculation of cost after losing a previous ticket than after losing a $20 bill.

Quantitative results have very limited significance in any case because the sample of participants does not represent more than a group of psychology, economics, or MBA students in a particular university. The qualitative results are usually insights that common sense had already suggested prior to the experiment. So why is there a need for experiments at all? Why is it not possible to suffice with self-reporting by researchers, as is customary in philosophy? For years I thought that experiments in economics were nothing but a waste of research funds. I still do not find great relevance in quantitative results, and I believe that the most reliable test of the reasonableness of an idea is that of common sense. But my appreciation of experiments grew after I realized that composing an array of questions that succeeds in illustrating a certain thought process is a work of art, and after I became convinced that common sense sometimes does deceive even the most experienced of us.

In recent years, I have myself been guilty of conducting experiments. I felt the captivating excitement when results started to arrive and a hypothesis became a proven fact, or the pervasive disappointment when it became apparent that "something went wrong here." I have never bet at horse races, but I imagine that the feelings of a researcher as the results of an experiment come in are similar to a gambler's feelings when the horses are racing round the track. And incidentally, the risk taken by researchers is no less than that of professional gamblers. At stake are the researcher's honor, satisfaction, professional advancement and the monetary compensation awarded to him.

My personal experience with experiments has led me to doubt the validity of the results of experiments in economics. Economists are not cheats, but like everyone else they make mistakes, for the most part unwittingly, and have a tendency to further their own interests. The economist wants his results to confirm his hypothesis. He is sure that he is right and the experiment is merely designed to confirm what he knows. He regards caution and meticulousness as unnecessary obstacles on the path of advancing human knowledge. I myself felt an urge to refrain from extending an experiment after the results I received in the initial stage were favorable, and I felt compelled to check the results seven times when they did not support a hypothesis I "knew" to be correct. The fear of being embarrassed if the conclusions are refuted by other researchers is almost non-existent in economics because we have no tradition of checking data and repeating experiments.

It is strange that according to the economic view of the world, people are economic agents who respond to incentives, primarily material ones. The economist describes them as aspiring to attain an objective that rates money, and perhaps status, highly, and gives a low rating to moral values. In this world view, all human beings are economic agents and their actions should be regarded from the perspective of their motives. All of them, except a group of angels who look at the world from above: the economists.

Rationality on the defensive

There are those who defend the assumption of rationality, arguing that behavior that appears to be irrational at first glance is indeed rational if only we define the decision problem correctly. Take for example the case in which we must choose one alternative from among a very large set of possibilities. What we normally do is we examine a relatively small number of options until we find an alternative that satisfies us. At that moment, we know that there might be better options than the one we are about to choose. Ostensibly, we are not acting rationally. We are not choosing the best alternative from among the set of choices. But it turns out that this pattern of behavior can be explained within the framework of the rational decision maker. In order to do this, one must describe the decision maker not only as someone who decides which alternative to choose, but rather as someone who also must decide when to bring the decision process to a close, taking into account the physical or mental demands the decision process entails.

There are those who justify the assumption of rationality by evolutionary considerations: if people in the world had used patterns of behavior that clash with rationality, a manipulator would have emerged to exploit their irrationality for his own benefit and to their detriment – until they realized this and changed their behavior or until they became extinct.

For example, consider a decision maker who is ready to pay a dollar to exchange object A for object B, and is ready to pay a dollar to exchange B for object C, and is ready to pay a dollar to exchange C for A. Let's also assume that he prefers more money to less money in his pocket. The decision maker is not rational: we cannot attribute to him an order of priorities that explains his behavior. If someone like this initially holds A and $1 million, he would be susceptible to a manipulator offering him a series of exchanges for a dollar. At first the manipulator would offer to exchange A for B for one dollar. After this offer was accepted, he would offer to trade B for C for one dollar, and then C for A for one dollar… and so on. Before long, our decision maker would wake up and change his behavior – and if not, he would find that his bank account had been depleted.

This is a fascinating argument for the assumption that individuals whose behavior is inconsistent with the assumption of rationality cannot survive for long. But it is not so obvious that such individuals would become extinct. The manipulators waste energy in hunting the irrational creatures, and may be expected to cease their activities before they destroy all their source of sustenance (or they may become extinct themselves). The survival of those who eradicate the irrational individuals requires the survival of their irrational victims. This is similar to the argument that in nature the fact that one creature is stronger than another and depends on it for food does not mean that the weaker creature will become extinct, but actually explains the mutual existence of both.

And there are those who approach the criticism of the assumption of rationality as if they were a labor union, arguing that the criticism is fundamentally destructive, that it does not offer alternative working frameworks and should therefore be ignored.

In recent years, economic theory has actually responded positively to criticism and we have witnessed the development of fields of research called "bounded rationality" and "behavioral economics" – fields that lay an infrastructure for building economic models in which the rational person is replaced by decision makers with other characteristics.

And do I want to be rational?

I refuse to answer this question rationalistically. That would require me to grapple with the meaning of life, to define the goals of my life, to clarify which paths of life are open to me, to face the certainty of death and to embrace maximization – which I have no idea how to describe, let alone solve. I prefer not to go down that route.

I can only say that I take pleasure in watching the rational man defeated. I do not like his perfection. The more I imagine him as flesh and blood, the more I realize that he is unbearable, even inhuman. The fact that this person does not actually exist – and that it is possible, using simple tricks, to make fun of anyone who considers himself rational – really makes me happy. I like the fact that I myself would make "problematic" choices in most of the problems I presented in this chapter. When explaining the concept of the rational man and discussing these issues in my economics courses, I make a point of saying that even after discerning the inconsistency in my behavior, I will continue to break all the rules and promise to violate the economic principles of rationality.

"Why?" I ask myself. First, I recoil from the aura of dogmatism emanating from the assumption of rationality in economics. I have a feeling that economics preaches that there is something that should be called correct behavior. That makes me feel as if I am denied the right to be myself and am forced into a mold designed to train me to behave as the economic models assume I behave. I refuse to obey.

Second, the assumption of rationality is supposed to make me predictable. I do not want someone to anticipate my moves and I do not want to be able to predict the activity of other people. I never understood why the world would be better if there were someone who knows what we will do before we do it. I am prepared to make significant sacrifices if only to do the opposite of what the perfect prophet predicts when he appears one day. And even if he tarries – I will wait for him. I so much want to defeat him.

Nonetheless, when all is said and done, I see myself as a very rational person, explaining every coincidence with statistical tools, refusing to recognize the existence of the hand of fate and supernatural forces.

2. Game Theory:
A Beautiful Mind

1973

I encountered the word Nash. I was a student at Hebrew University in Jerusalem and I came across Nash in an introductory Game Theory course. For me, Nash was then just a short and catchy adjective attached to two abstract concepts that are central to game theory: **Nash Equilibrium** and the **Nash Bargaining Solution**. If the concept of equilibrium were named Cournot (who had already thought of this concept in a narrow context in 1838) or "Alpha Equilibrium" or even "Smiley," it would really have made no difference to me. I must have realized that the word Nash was connected to a person. And if I had asked myself who Nash was, I probably would have guessed he was an English intellectual who died at the beginning of the twentieth century.

Autumn 1980

I arrived at Princeton for the first time. I heard from other students that a crazy genius would roam around the campus, sitting for hours in the cafeteria with a pile of computer printouts in front of him, reading newspapers he collected from abandoned tables. This crazy person could be seen riding back and forth on the "Dinky," a short rail line connecting Princeton Junction to the campus. It was rumored that he had an account on the university's computer and was busy with mysterious calculations. They said there was one student who had dared to approach him and speak with him, and that he had readily helped the student. It was hard for me to identify him; a lot of weird people roam the lawns at Princeton.

One afternoon, I was about to give a lecture in the Economics Department. Before the lecture, I asked my host to take me to the cafeteria and show me this ethereal character. My host looked toward one of the tables, lowered his eyes and whispered to me: "That's John Nash." The man whose name rolled off my tongue more often than any other name in my professional life and whose work was the basis for the bargaining model I was about to present that day, was hunched over the table, wrapped in a long and shabby coat, wearing worn-out sneakers, and not looking at anyone. He was a solitary figure in the cafeteria, which looked like a dining hall in an Oxford college. I did not approach him, of course. I was not merely shy; I was afraid to speak with someone who was crazy.

Game theory

Whoever invented the name "game theory" was also a genius in public relations. Who would be interested in this theory if it were called "A Collection of Models of Rational Decision-Making in Interactive Situations"?

The word "game" has a mischievous, youthful and accessible ring to it. We all play board games, social games, political games and other games. Add to this the fact that the basic terminology of game theory includes words like "strategy" and "solution," and it becomes a real celebration. After all, we are all frustrated experts in war strategy and everyone is searching for a solution to the conflict in the Middle East. So here, maybe, just maybe, we have found the lost box of tricks with the hidden secrets that will improve our game skills. But it is not quite so simple. I will try to explain, but first I will reiterate that some of the things I am going to say here are not uncontroversial.

I think that the body of knowledge called game theory is a collection of formal models that enables us to analyze strategic and rational patterns of human thought. It sounds terrible, so I will elaborate a bit.

In game theory, as in most economic theories, the operating units are rational decision makers. The decision maker, who is called a **player** in game theory, seeks to attain a well-defined objective. Whenever he is required to carry out an activity, he behaves (or at least can be regarded as behaving) in the following way: he asks himself what is desirable and what is possible, and does what is best in his (subjective) view, given what is possible (objectively speaking).

Not every decision problem is a game theory problem. Let's say that I am about to leave my house and I am contemplating whether or not to take an umbrella. I have four possible scenarios in mind: "I have an umbrella and

it's raining," "I have an umbrella and it isn't raining," "I
don't have an umbrella and it's raining," and "I don't
have an umbrella and it isn't raining." I have some sense
of how much pleasure or discomfort I would experience
in each of the four situations. Whatever I decide the
outcome is uncertain, which in our professional jargon
we call a lottery. If I take an umbrella with me, there is
a chance I will find myself opening it and will stay dry,
and there is also a possibility that I will drag it with me
for no reason. If I do not take an umbrella, there is a
chance that I will get wet, and there is also a chance that
I will be able to enjoy strolling around without having
to schlep an umbrella around. I assess the chance of rain,
something I have no control over that is determined by
nature, compare the two possibilities, and decide. I do
not have to predict anyone's action or imagine anyone
else's calculations. It is just me, alone. I face a decision
problem that is not a game.

On the other hand, let's say that I believe there is a
rain god up above who holds the key to the floodgates
of heaven and that this rain god has interests of his own.
Maybe he cares about me, but maybe he really doesn't
like me, and has it in for me. My forecast of the rain god's
behavior will be based not only on the meteorological
service, but also on an analysis of the god's considerations.
Maybe he will want me to get caught in a heavy storm if
I make light of his powers and ignore threatening skies.
And maybe if I believe in his being merciful and leave
the house without an umbrella he will reward my faith in
him by scattering the clouds.

Or, let's say that I plan to go for a romantic walk in the rain under one umbrella with a friend, who will be coming from her home, and that she too must decide whether to take an umbrella when she leaves her house. My rational decision will be affected by my expectations of my friend's behavior and my expectations will be based, among other things, on the fact that both of us dream of walking in the rain under one umbrella.

In such situations, I must exercise **strategic thought**: I ask myself what the rain god (or my friend) will do. My expectations develop as I ask myself how they analyze the situation and what they think about me. Game theory deals with situations in which each of the players is a rational decision maker and puts himself in the shoes of the other before making a decision.

March 2002

I brought my son Yuval to the first meeting of the beginners' group of a chess class. The veteran Tel Aviv teacher who directed the activity began with a direct appeal to the children. She encouraged the children, who came from various neighborhoods, to become friends and added, with feeling: "Children, I think chess is very important because it teaches you to look at other children from their point of view." I said to myself: what a nice approach she has, teaching the children to think about others through the game of chess. I recalled the words of the game theorist, John McMillan, in the summary of a chapter on negotiating:

> What advice for negotiators does Game Theory generate?
> The most important ideas we have learned... are the
> value of putting yourself in the other person's shoes and
> looking several moves ahead.

I was excited – I recognized game theory in the words of a children's teacher. But after the initial excitement, I wondered: game theory and the game of chess perhaps encourage a person to think about a situation from the perspective of the other, but only in order to do the best thing for himself. The chess teacher confused strategic thinking with developing empathy. Strategic thinking does not encourage a person to think about the wellbeing of the other. Game theory speaks of a player who steps into the shoes of the other in order to assess what the other will do, and he does this for his own benefit, in accordance with his own preferences. But these preferences may reflect affection, sympathy and benevolence, or hatred, bitterness and revenge. An educational task such as developing empathy remains in the realm of the kindergarten teacher, not the chess teacher and not the expert in game theory.

The Traveler's Dilemma

Let's play (you can experiment with the situations discussed here and in the rest of the chapter: http://www.openbookpublishers.com/exsites/136). Here is a well-known situation called the Traveler's Dilemma or Basu's Game. Originally, it involved a story about two travelers returning from the same holiday resort, both bringing the same souvenir in their suitcases. The suitcases are lost and the lost-baggage clerk at the airport must compensate them for the real value of the loss. The clerk has only a vague idea of the value of the lost object: between $180 and $300. Therefore, he plans to award compensation according to the declarations of the two travelers, but he knows they are liable to exaggerate the value of the loss and that they do not feel obliged to tell the truth. He takes the two travelers into separate rooms and asks each of them to declare the value of the souvenir – an amount between $180 and $300. He promises to compensate both of them according to the lower of the two values they declare. In addition, if they give different prices, he will impose a "fine" of $5 on the traveler who states the higher price and will "award a prize" of $5 to the traveler whose demand is more modest.

In order to consider this situation in terms of game theory, we must answer several questions:

1. Who are the players?
2. For each player, what choices does he face? (We sometimes call these choices: "strategies.")
3. For each combination of choices by the players, what will be the result of the game? (Unlike non-game decision problems, the consequence of a player's decision does not depend solely on the action he chooses. It depends also on the actions the other players choose.)
4. For each player, what are his preferences? (That is, how does he rank the possible results of the game?)

Only after answering all of these questions can we say that we have defined the story as a **game** in the accepted sense of game theory.

In the case of the Traveler's Dilemma, the answers to the four questions are:

1. The players are the two travelers.
2. For each player, the possible choices are amounts between $180 and $300.
3. Each player receives a number of dollars equal to the smaller of the two numbers chosen by the players, plus $5 if the number he chooses is lower than the number the other player chooses, or minus $5 if the number he chooses is higher than the number the other player chooses.
4. Each player is interested in receiving as much money as possible.

The answer we gave to the fourth question does not derive from the initial description of the situation. The need to answer all of the questions made us describe the players' preferences. In answering the fourth question, we assumed that each player is only interested in the amount of money he will receive at the end of the game, and that he is not interested in what the other player receives or the ratio between the two sums. This assumption is not obvious and is probably not realistic. Game theory certainly allows for an analysis of this situation even when we attribute additional considerations to the players, such as "I do not want to be seen as petty in trying to earn a few dollars at the other guy's expense," "It is important to me that both of us together receive as much as possible," or "I do not want to be the sucker of that smart-aleck." But in game theory, an unfortunate convention has taken root: when we state that game theory says the outcome of the game will be this or that, we assume that the only thing a player cares about is the amount of money he will receive at the end of the game.

Clearly, each player faces a strategic decision here. The best action from one player's perspective depends on what he expects the other player to do. The rationality of a player is defined in game theory as choosing the best action in light of his beliefs about the behavior of the other players. This definition does not impose constraints on these beliefs and, in particular, does not demand that the beliefs be reasonable in any sense.

In the current case of the Traveler's Dilemma, it seems that the choice of $300 is not rational for me as a player in the game. Regardless of what I believe the other player will do, there is another declaration of price that would result in my receiving more than $300. If I believe that the other player will choose $300, my choice of $300 would bring me $300, while if I chose $299 I would receive $304. And if I believe that he will choose a number N, which is less than 300, then the choice of $300 would compensate me with only $(N-5), while if I choose the number N, for example, I would receive $N.

Even if I am not sure about the other player's price declaration, the action $300 cannot be rational.

Let's assume that I am certain that he will choose a number no greater than M, and that I attribute a positive probability to both of the other possibilities: that he will choose exactly M or a number less than M. We will show now that choosing the number M-1 is preferable to choosing the number 300. To be precise, we will show that there are circumstances in which declaring M-1 would yield a higher sum than declaring 300, and that there are no circumstances in which declaring 300 would yield higher revenue than declaring M-1. If the other player declares M and I declare M-1, I will receive $M+4. And if I declare 300, I will receive at most $M. If the other player chooses M-1 and I do the same, I will receive $M-1 and that is more than the $M-6 I would receive if I choose 300. Finally, if the other player chooses a number less than M-1, the payment I receive will be the same regardless of whether I choose M-1 or 300.

So we have rejected the rationality of choosing $300. Could it be rational from my perspective to choose the number $299? Yes. For example, if I am sure the other player will choose the number 300, it will be best for me to choose 299. But if I put myself in the shoes of the other player and assume that he also is rational, I will reach the conclusion that he will surely refrain from choosing the number 300 too. Thus, the highest number he might choose is 299. Consequently, following the principle of the previous argument, the choice of 299 is also not a rational choice for me. And if I again put myself in the shoes of the other player and assume that he puts himself in my shoes, I will reach the conclusion that he believes I will not choose 300 and, therefore, he will also refrain from choosing the number 299. Accordingly, the choice of 298 is also not rational from my perspective. And now, in order to decide what is good for me, I must step into the shoes of the other and think how he puts himself in my shoes and imagines my stepping into his shoes. It is difficult for me to keep track of this reasoning. This circular thinking simply drives me crazy. It is like the sentence: "I think that she does not think that I think that she will smile at me if I go up to her." It is a proper sentence and has meaning, but it is annoying.

Nash equilibrium: In the introductory chapter, we said that a solution concept is an array of rules by which an economic tale is allowed to develop from its beginning to its end. In the context of game theory, the beginning of the tale is a description of the game, and its end is the actions the players choose. Nash equilibrium is a solution concept that extricates us from the whirlpool of "I think that he thinks that I think…" The concept is built upon two assumptions:

First, the action attributed to a player is the best for him in light of what he believes the other players will do.

Second, the player's belief regarding the actions of the other players is correct.

In other words, according to Nash, the answer to the question "What will happen?" is consistent with the assumption that each individual is able to step into the other's shoes, correctly predict his moves, return to his own shoes and choose the best action from there.

There are also other interpretations of Nash equilibrium. For example, sometimes we think of Nash equilibrium as a stable norm of behavior. A norm of behavior is a rule that tells individuals what to do in the various situations they are liable to encounter. A norm of behavior in a game situation is stable if the action prescribed by the norm for each player is the best one for him when he expects the other players to act according to the same norm. In other words, a stable norm of behavior is a rule of behavior that advises the players in the game to act in accordance with Nash equilibrium. For example, in the context of the Traveler's Dilemma, the norm of asking for as much as you can is not stable because it is worthwhile for each individual to deviate from the norm and to demand a bit less. (The slightly more modest demand is rewarded with an extra payment.) On the other hand, the norm of being as modest as possible in your demands is stable in this game.

Nash was not the first one to use the concept of equilibrium, but he was the first to formulate it in an abstract way and not in the context of a specific game. There is no guarantee that a Nash equilibrium exists in a game; there are games that do not have an equilibrium. Nash showed that if a game meets certain conditions, a Nash equilibrium does indeed exist. This is the original mathematical part of his work.

Back to Basu and the travelers: what is the Nash equilibrium in Basu's Game? One player chooses $250 and the second chooses $240 – this is not an equilibrium. When the second player declares $240, it is not optimal for the first player to declare $250. The first player can receive higher compensation if he chooses, for example, $239. Similarly, there is no equilibrium in which the two players choose any two different numbers.

If both of the players choose $240, this is also not an equilibrium. Each player can enlarge his payoff by subtracting a dollar from his demand. Similarly, there is no equilibrium in which both players choose another identical number. There is only one exception and it is when both players choose $180. One cannot go lower.

Choosing $180 is the best for a player who believes that the other player will choose $180.

Conclusion: The Traveler's Dilemma has a unique equilibrium in which both players choose $180. We asked: "What will happen?" And here, in this game, the Nash equilibrium gives us an unequivocal answer. (Incidentally, this is quite a rare situation.) Hallelu-Nash.

How is the answer the Nash equilibrium provides in this game related to human behavior in reality? We do not know how people would behave in such a situation in real life. At best, it is possible to bring people to a laboratory and watch them play a similar game. This would be a costly experiment. Alternatively, it is possible to ask people, like the readers of this book, to imagine themselves in this type of situation. People are quite imaginative and like to play such games. The participants can be encouraged to take the game seriously by awarding a symbolic payment. In my view, as I already noted in the previous chapter, such a reward is completely unnecessary and may even be detrimental.

I have data on the responses of more than 13,000 people who were asked to answer (via the website http://gametheory. tau.ac.il) the question of what they would do if they were players in the game. One third of the respondents were students in game theory courses in about thirty countries, and half were people invited to eleven public lectures on "Game Theory and John Nash" that I delivered in recent years in seven countries. Before each lecture, I asked the audience to answer a number of questions, including those in Basu's Game. Of course, the sample is not representative of the world's population. But our objective is not to describe, even approximately, how the world's population plays the game. Our interest is to peek into the considerations of the people participating in this game, and we would be happy to get even a rough impression of how common these considerations are world wide.

Among the respondents, 45% chose the price $300, a choice we have just termed irrational. Only 20% of the respondents chose $180, the choice recommended by the concept of Nash equilibrium. Another 19% chose between $295 and $299, while the choices of the remaining 16% were in the broad range of $181 to $294.

The players who chose a number in the range of 295 to 299 apparently used strategic thinking. That is, they said to themselves something like: The other player will choose 298, so I will choose 297, or to be sure I'll even go down to 296. On what basis do I determine that the respondents in this range were more strategic than the respondents who chose a number from 181 to 294? First, I do this based on introspection: I can find a reasonable explanation for the choice of 297, but cannot find one for choosing a number such as 236. And I also have additional support for the assumption that the choice of a number in the range of 295 to 299 is the outcome of more serious thinking: I also recorded the **response time** of the participants in the experiment – that is, the time from the moment the computer sent them the question until it received their answer. The response time of those whose choice was in the range of 295 to 299 was significantly greater (a median of 107 seconds) than the response time of those quoting in the range of 181–294 and of those who chose the number 300 (a median of 77 seconds).

I suspect that most of the respondents who chose the number 180 are members of the Victims of Game

Theory organization, who implemented the concept of Nash equilibrium without exercising common sense. If you had to play against a randomly selected participant in the experiment, I would not recommend that you choose an equilibrium action. According to the rules of the game, you will be able to win a maximum of $185. On the other hand, a simple calculation shows that if you choose 298 or 299, and you play against one of the subjects in my database you can expect to receive an average payment of $262.

And here is another interesting fact: The distributions of the answers in various countries (among audiences at my public lectures) were similar.

Traveler's Dilema
Distribution of declared values

	Netherlands	Israel	UK	Canada	USA	Thailand
Number of Participants :	613	687	656	648	957	422
Average Declaration :	278	278	281	272	275	251

I have no substantiated explanation for this fact. Perhaps people are divided into different types and their type determines their choice in this game. For example, perhaps there are four types: the instinctive (who chooses the number 300 in this game); the sophisticated (who chooses a number in the range of 295–299); the disciplined (who took a course in game theory and, obeying the equilibrium, chooses 180); and the capricious (who chooses a number randomly). And perhaps every society has a similar distribution of these four types. Of course, this is a far-reaching hypothesis that I cannot substantiate. If this hypothesis were firmly based, we would expect that we could assess the distribution of types and estimate the distribution of behaviors in various games.

Despite the fact that the distributions of answers in the seven countries are similar, there are also significant differences, particularly in the percentage of those choosing the game theory solution, 180. This fact is perhaps related to the percentage of respondents who had taken a course in game theory. I find support for this assumption in the results from 9,300 students in game theory courses who were presented with the same question. The percentage of those choosing the equilibrium action was 23%, compared with 14% in the more diverse population of those attending public lectures on game theory. This increase in the share was derived primarily from a decline in the percentage of those choosing 300. This outcome strengthens the suspicion that a small group of students had internalized the ideas presented in the game theory course, even to the point of choosing the equilibrium point when this action was not really the most intelligent thing to do.

Does Basu's Game show that the concept of Nash equilibrium *does not* explain the way people play? Not necessarily. Nash equilibrium is a **solution concept** applied to a description of a game that includes not only the procedure of the game, but also the preferences of the players. We saw that the popular choice of the maximum number, 300, is not rational if the players care only about the sum of money they will receive at the end of the game. But the choice of $300 can be optimal for a player whose preferences include considerations such as unpleasantness about profiting at the expense of others or embarrassment for appearing to be petty. Therefore, the norm of behavior of seeking to collaborate with the other player, expressed in this game by choosing $300, is not a Nash equilibrium if the players care only about the cash in their pocket, but this norm is stable in the sense of Nash equilibrium if the players' preferences are such that the unpleasantness caused to a player who made a few dollars at the expense of the other player is the same as losing more than $4.

The Ultimatum Game

Here is another game. Two individuals, who are capable of reaching an agreement, participate in the Ultimatum Game. There are several possible agreements that they would prefer to accept rather than remain in disagreement. Some of the agreements are better for one player and others are better for the other player. One of the players in the game is assigned the role of the **proposer** and the second player is the **responder**. The proposer must offer a proposal for an agreement and the responder must accept or reject the proposal. If the responder accepts the proposal, the agreement is executed. If the responder rejects the proposal, the two players part ways without an agreement.

Ultimatum games are common in everyday life: in the labor market, unskilled workers can only say yes or no when offered a job. They usually say yes even when offered meager wages. In every visit to the supermarket, you are actually participating in an ultimatum game. You want a carton of milk. The supermarket places an ultimatum before you – either buy it at the set price or don't buy it. There is no point in arguing with the cashier at the supermarket about the price of milk. Sometimes the situation occurs not in real life, but rather in the imagination of someone who believes that he can make the other side an offer he cannot refuse. How disappointed he is when it turns out that he was mistaken in his in assessment of the considerations of the other side.

To keep it simple, we will focus on an ultimatum game involving $100. The agreement is any allocation of the sum between the two individuals. If there is no agreement, the two individuals will receive nothing. In order to complete the description of the situation, we must describe the preferences of the players. And again, as usual, we will assume (something that is not self-evident) that each player is only concerned with the sum of money he gets at the end of the game, and that he is interested in getting as much as possible.

As always, in order to analyze the game, we must apply a solution concept. For this type of game, the conventional practice in economics is to apply a solution concept called **perfect equilibrium**. This is a version of Nash equilibrium, adapted for games involving a series of moves. We will now apply this concept, which was discussed in the opening chapter of the book, to the Ultimatum Game. A perfect equilibrium describes a pair of plans of action, one for the proposer and one for the responder. The proposer's plan of action is the proposal he intends to offer to the responder. The responder's plan of action is a policy that describes which proposals he will accept and which he will reject. Perfect equilibrium demands that the pair of plans of action meet two requirements. The first requirement pertains to the proposer's plan of action: the proposal he intends to offer to the responder must be the best one for the proposer, taking into account the responder's policy of acceptance. The second requirement pertains to the responder's plan of action: if the responder intends to accept a certain proposal, he would not benefit by rejecting it; and if the responder intends to reject a certain proposal, it would not be preferable for him to accept it. In other words, after each proposal that the proposer might offer (and not only the proposal he is supposed to offer according to his plan of action), the responder's plan of response is best for him.

Here is one perfect equilibrium of the game. The proposer's plan: offer $1 to the responder. The responder's plan: accept any offer except $0. Now let's check whether the plan of each player is optimal in every possible scenario in which he is likely to implement it.

The proposer starts the game. His decision problem is to choose one of 101 possible proposals. According to the responder's strategy, each proposal of a positive number of dollars, X, will be accepted and is "worth" $100-X to the proposer. The proposal $0 will be rejected and is therefore worth $0 to the proposer. Thus, the best action for the proposer is indeed to offer $1 to the responder.

The responder will have to act after receiving the proposal. If the proposal is a positive sum, it is best for him to accept it, because rejecting it would mean receiving nothing. If the proposal is $0, then he would be left with the same $0 regardless of whether he accepts or rejects the proposal. Therefore, rejecting the proposal, as planned, is an optimal action from his perspective.

It is easy to confirm that the game also has a second perfect equilibrium in which the proposer offers $0 and the responder plans to say yes to any proposal offered to him, including the insulting offer of $0.

We will now see that in every perfect equilibrium the proposer ends the game with at least $99. In other words, there is no perfect equilibrium in which the proposer receives less than $99. Accepting any proposal that gives the responder at least $1 is better for him than the alternative of rejecting the proposal and receiving nothing. Therefore, in every perfect equilibrium, the responder plans to accept every offer that gives him at least $1 and, consequently, the proposer can receive at least $99. In a perfect equilibrium, the proposer chooses an optimal plan and it awards him at least $99.

Let's summarize: game theory "predicts" what many people think. The player who is able to issue an ultimatum has a great advantage over the player who can only accept or reject the proposal. The first player will receive all (or almost all) of the pie that is to be allocated.

The Ultimatum Game and its analysis by means of the concept of perfect equilibrium serve as a basis for many other and more complex economic models. I know very few games that have been given so much attention. Is the outcome of the model consistent with behavior in real life? This question has been examined in various experiments in many cultures – with money, with lots of money and without money – and with a large number of participants. On the book's website, the Ultimatum Game is expressed in this way:

> Imagine you and someone you do not know can share $100. It is up to you to propose how to divide the $100 between the two of you, and the other player will need to accept or reject your proposal. If he rejects the proposal, neither of you will receive anything.
>
> What sum will you offer the other player?

I have data on the choices of about 12,300 people, most of them students, who were asked this question. Nearly half of the participants (49%) offered the other player the fair offer of $50. About 9% took advantage of their position to some extent and offered the other player a sum in the range of $40 to $49 – that is, just a little less than $50. Some 12% offered the other player only $1 (and only 1% made the even more absurd offer of $0). And 13% offered the responder a sum in the broad range of $2 to $39.

One group, not mentioned above, stood out: the 18% of the participants who offer the other player more than $50. Some of them apparently got confused between receiving and giving – for example, writing the number 60 and expecting to receive $60 if this offer was accepted. But the fact that 7% of the proposers offered a proposal in the range of 51 to 59 (compared to only 3% who made an offer in the parallel range of 41 to 49) suggests that there is a significant group of "annoyingly" generous people who feel better if they receive less than what they are entitled to under the conventional rules of fairness.

Ultimatum Game
Distribution of Proposals

	Netherlands	Israel	UK	Canada	USA	Thailand

Number of Participants :	655	720	680	694	1055	519
Average Proposal :	40	44	42	44	45	48
Male :	40	43	40	43	43	48
Female :	44	46	45	46	47	48

The figure presents distributions of the proposals of nearly 5,000 people invited to public lectures on game theory in seven countries. The distributions are similar, but there are also differences. I might be tempted to say that the Dutch are tougher than the Israelis because the Dutch, on average, offer $4 less than the Israelis. I might also be impressed by the fact that the highest percentage of those offering the fair allocation is in the U.S. (59%). But I do not attribute significance to these findings: at most, they are interesting observations. One result that is perhaps more significant pertains to the differences between the genders: in nearly all of the universities, the average proposal by women was higher by $3 to $5 than that of men. Some 56% of the women chose the fair allocation, compared to only 46% of the men. No more than 8% of the women offered a proposal consistent with the game theory solution, compared to 14% of the men. In other words, the women are more generous and less attracted to the game theory analysis.

What would people do as responders? The following question also appears on the book's website:

> You and a person you do not know can share $100. He offers a proposal and you can only accept or reject it. If you reject it, both of you will receive nothing.
>
> He offers you $10 (and if you accept the offer, he will receive $90).
>
> Would you accept the offer?

I have the responses of 8,100 participants. Some 63% of them accepted the proposal. The percentage of those accepting the proposal ranged from 52% in Bangkok to 72% in Tel Aviv. If I took the results of the survey seriously (and I do not), I would predict, based on these data, that a large number of Israelis would acquiesce to an international ultimatum to return more or less to the 1967 borders. (As a matter of fact, I think this is true – not because of these data, but based on my familiarity with Israeli society.) And another finding related to gender: about 60% of the women accepted the offer of $10, compared with 65% of the men. Are women tougher? Are they less materialistic? Or are they endowed with a more developed sense of fairness? In any case, in my view they are more pleasant.

As is customary in economic models, at least until recent times, the classic analysis of the game assumes that each player is interested only in the sum of money he himself will receive at the end of the game. Is this description of the players' preferences in the game correct? It is very doubtful.

First, many people also show interest in a fair allocation and not only in the sum of money they receive. There are even those who are happier if the sum of money is split equally between the two players than if they receive the entire sum. A situation the literature calls the **Dictator Game** clearly reveals the existence of these considerations. In the Dictator Game, one player – called the dictator – is asked to divide a sum of money between himself and another anonymous player. The other party plays no active role in the game, so it is actually a decision problem. Thousands of students in game theory courses were asked to imagine a situation in which they play the game as the dictator. About 36% took the entire sum, about 35% divided the sum equally between them and the anonymous player, and nearly all of the others allocated something to the other player, but less than the sum they allocated to themselves. On average, the dictator gave the other player about a quarter of the sum to be allocated. These facts indicate that in such situations most people are not so selfish and also consider the fairness of the allocation.

People care not only about the sums of money they will receive at the end of a game, but also about the way they obtain the money. Let's say that $100 is about to fall from the sky, with $10 falling into my hands and $90 into the hands of my neighbor, and I have the ability to prevent this shower of dollars. The choice I face is between the allocation of $10 to me and $90 to the neighbor, or a situation in which both of us receive nothing. I would be considered malicious if I preferred that we both receive nothing rather than my neighbor receiving much more than I do. On the other hand, let's say that in the Ultimatum Game I receive an offer of $10, which leaves $90 in the hands of my brazen neighbor, the proposer. In this case, I would undoubtedly surrender the $10 as long as it would put the proposer in his place. I thought that nearly everyone feels like me, but to my surprise only about a half of the respondents in the survey declared that they would reject the proposal to receive $10 out of the $100.

It goes without saying that I would not use classic game theory analysis as a basis for advising a person who is about to deliver an ultimatum demanding "all" or "nearly all" of the pie. There is reason to believe that at least 75% of the participants would reject the offer of $1 and that (almost) everyone would accept the 50–50 offer. Thus, a proposer who acts according to the recommendation of game theory would receive $0 in 75% of the cases and the average (expected) number of dollars in his pocket would be less than $25. If he acts in a less sophisticated way and proposes the fair allocation, he would almost certainly receive an affirmative response and could expect to have nearly $50 in his pocket. The participants in the experiment who make the embarrassing offer of just $1 because they learned this in a game theory course are again the distinguished members of the Victims of Game Theory organization. And if they played the game in real life, their achievements would be inferior to those who had not become wise by studying game theory.

This does not prevent some strategic experts from treating the game theory solution of the Ultimatum

Game as a sacred rule. Some say that a certain prime minister of Israel issued an ultimatum to the head of the Palestinian Authority that granted the Palestinians 90% of the territory of the West Bank and Gaza Strip. The *rais* refused and the rest is written in another bloody page in the chronicles of the Middle East. When the other side believes that it deserves 100% or that the pie is part of another pie and 90% of the small pie is less than 50% of the large pie, it is likely to reject even an offer of 90% of the small pie.

Autumn 1985

I was a young, fresh lecturer in the Department of Economics in Jerusalem. One day, a letter from the Nobel Prize Committee landed in my mailbox. I was surprised. I later understood that the selection committee for the prize was seeking to identify important fields and worthy candidates by approaching researchers who were in the early stages of their careers. I began my response to the committee's query with banal remarks about the centrality of game theory in economic theory. I listed many fields in which game theory is used. When I came to candidates, I cited four names. And then, I added a paragraph on a fifth candidate, John Nash. I wrote that Nash, the outstanding person in the group, lives in Princeton and had stopped working due to personal problems, but that the three articles he wrote during 1950 to 1953 were the most important and most inspiring in game theory and in all of economic theory since the book *Theory of Games and Economic Behavior* by John von Neumann and Oskar Morgenstern. Nash was clearly worthy of the Nobel Prize. My remarks had at most a marginal influence on his winning the prize nine years later. And I was left to wonder: was I motivated only by academic judgment or did I also want to rectify the injustice suffered by someone who had been abandoned and had not received the recognition he would have gained if he had not been mentally ill? Is it possible and is it desirable to separate the goal of correcting human injustice from pure academic assessment?

Hotelling's Game

Let's return to the games. The next game, in a slightly different form, was discussed in the introductory chapter.

Imagine that you are the manager of a chain of coffee shops competing against two other chains. A new beachfront residential neighborhood is being built, with seven huge apartment blocks equal in size and equidistant from one another. The towers are numbered from left to right: 1, 2, 3, 4, 5, 6, 7.

Each of the three chains plans to open a branch in one of the blocks. The three coffee shops will be very similar. The manager of each of the chains must decide in which block to open a branch, with the goal of attracting as many customers as possible. He must make a decision immediately, before knowing where his two competitors will set up their coffee shops.

The clientele is expected to consist of residents of the seven blocks and each customer is expected to patronize the cafe that is closest to his apartment.

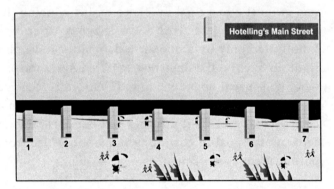

In which block will you set up the coffee shop of the chain you manage?

Hotelling spoke about a main street and stores. Here, the main street becomes seven blocks on a beachfront and the stores become coffee shops. I admit that this is an expression of my fondness for coffee shops. While I try to boycott the coffee chains that annihilate the intimate neighborhood coffee shops that I love so much, I have compromised here in order to make the story more realistic.

The assumptions in the story are reasonable, even if they do not perfectly describe reality. In real life, coffee shops are not absolutely identical. Some people prefer to patronize a particular coffee shop even if it is further from where they live. The coffee shops in our game compete with their rivals only in terms of location, while in reality competition is frequently conducted via the price and quality of the coffee. We assume that the decisions are made simultaneously: each player chooses his location without knowing the location of the other two. In real life, the players try to preempt their rivals or, conversely, wait until the picture becomes clearer.

Let's assume first that only two (and not three) chains are competing in our example, and proceed to translate the story into a game. The two players in the game are the managers of the chains. Each chain must choose a tower, a number from 1 to 7. The chain's objective is to maximize the number of its clients, a number that depends on its location and the location of the other chain and is calculated as follows: for each block, we will check which chain has the nearest cafe and we will count the residents of the block as clients of that chain. If the two cafes are located at an equal distance from the tower, the residents of the tower will divide equally between them. For example, if Chain A opens a branch in Tower 4 and Chain B opens a branch in Tower 6, the residents of Towers 1, 2, 3, 4 will be customers of Chain A and the residents of Towers 6 and 7 will be customers of Chain B, while the residents of Tower 5 will be split between the two chains. In this case, Chain A's market share will consist of the residents of 4.5 towers, and the market share of Chain B will consist of the residents of 2.5 towers.

With two players in the game, there is a single Nash equilibrium: when both of the players set up their coffee shops in the middle block (No. 4). A unilateral move by one of the players from the center will diminish his clientele. The proof that there is no other equilibrium is similar to the one we saw in the introductory chapter: a situation in which one or more blocks separate the two cafes is not an equilibrium because if either of them moves to one of the blocks located between them, it would increase its market share. If the two cafes are located in adjacent towers, one of them enjoys less than half of the market and if it moves to the block in which the competitor is located, it would increase its market share to 50%. If the two cafes are located in the same block, and it is not the middle one, then each of them enjoys half of the market and can increase its share to at least 4/7 of the market by moving to the middle block.

Indeed, if I asked the readers to consider the game with two competitors, I am sure that an overwhelming majority would choose to locate in the middle block, thus confirming the game theory prediction. I have the results of a survey conducted among 8,100 participants. About 68% of them chose No. 4. This sounds like good news for those who look to game theory to help predict what will happen in real life. As I noted in the opening chapter, this game is important and resembles familiar real life situations. In as early as 1929, Hotelling said the following about the two players choosing to locate themselves in the middle:

> So general is this tendency that it appears in the most diverse fields of competitive activity, even quite apart from what is called economic life. In politics it is strikingly exemplified. The competition for votes between the Republican and Democratic parties does not lead to a clear drawing of issues, an adoption of two strongly contrasted positions between which the voter may choose. Instead, each party strives to make its platform as much like the other's as possible.

But... our joy is premature. What happens if three competitors, instead of two, operate on the beachfront?

It is not difficult to see that Hotelling's Game with three players does not have a Nash equilibrium. I will just explain here why locating the three cafes in the middle tower is not an equilibrium. If a player thinks that his two competitors will choose to locate their shops in No. 4, then his choice to locate his shop there will bring him a third of the total number of residents in the neighborhood. That is, the number of his customers will be equal to the number of residents in 2⅓ blocks. On the other hand, if he opens a shop in No. 3 or 5, his market share will be the residents of 3 blocks. Thus, the choice of No. 4 is not optimal for a player who anticipates that his two competitors will locate in the center. Therefore, setting up all three cafes in the middle block is not a Nash equilibrium.

Hotelling's Game with three players is a symmetrical game in the sense that the description of the game does not discriminate between the players. In games of this type, it is customary to look at the concept called **symmetric equilibrium**, an extension of the concept of Nash equilibrium. One can think of this kind of equilibrium as the distribution of behaviors in a large population of individuals, with each individual programmed to play the game in a specific way. The distribution of behaviors describes the percentage of individuals in a population who would choose Block No. 1 in the game, the percentage who would choose No. 2, and so on. Each individual in the population is programmed to locate himself in a particular apartment block and expects to play the game against two random competitors from within the population. In a symmetric equilibrium, none of the individuals programmed to set up in a certain block would be able to increase his anticipated market share by moving to another one.

Let's look at the following distribution of behaviors: Half of the population is programmed to choose Block No. 3 and the other half is programmed to choose No. 5.

A player who must decide where to locate his shop and knows that his competitors will be randomly selected from this distribution faces uncertainty regarding the location of his two competitors. He expects a probability of ¼ that both will locate their shops in No. 3, a probability of ¼ that both will locate their shops in No. 5, and a probability of ½ that one competitor will set up in No. 3 and the other in No. 5. Therefore, if he locates his shop in No. 4, there is a probability of ¼ that his clientele will include the residents of blocks 4, 5 ,6, 7; a probability of ¼ that his clientele will include the residents of Blocks 1, 2, 3, 4 ; and a probability of ½ that his clientele will only include the residents of No, 4. Consequently, the average market share of a player who locates his shop in No. 4 is equal to the number of residents in 2.5 blocks. On the other hand, the choice of No. 3 or No. 5 leads to an average clientele of the residents of only 7/3 blocks. (This is evident for reasons of symmetry, even without doing the calculation.)

All of this demonstrates that when a player expects that his two competitors are randomly selected from this population, the average market share he receives if he locates his shop in Block No. 4 will be greater than the average market share he can expect if he chooses what he was programmed to do. Therefore, this distribution is not a symmetrical equilibrium.

It is possible to show (and this demands a little work) that Hotelling's Game with three players has only one symmetric equilibrium, when 40% of the players choose No. 3, 20% choose No. 4 and 40% choose No. 5.

The following table presents the equilibrium distribution, alongside the distribution of choices of 7,400 people, most of them students in economics and game theory courses:

Tower	1	2	3	4	5	6	7
Equilibrium			40%	20%	40%		
Survey distribution	5%	8%	16%	43%	14%	8%	6%

As the game theory solution predicts, the proportion choosing the middle tower, 43%, is significantly lower than the proportion choosing this tower in Hotelling's Game with two stores, 70%. But there is no similarity between the distribution predicted by game theory and the distribution in the survey. The choice of the middle tower remains the most common even in a game with three players. This choice reflects the instinct (which we already noted in the previous chapter) of people when faced with a linear group of alternatives to choose the alternative in the center. An examination of the participants' response times supports the hypothesis that the choice of the middle tower is the instinctive action. The median response time (54 seconds) of the participants who chose Tower 4 is similar to the median response time of the individuals who chose the towers at the end of the line, which is clearly an irrational choice. On the other hand, the median response time of those who chose Towers 2, 3, 5, 6 was much higher (80 seconds).

The rise of game theory

Despite the lack of agreement between Nash equilibrium and the experimental evidence, game theory has become established as a central tool in economics. Nash equilibrium became an accepted solution concept that is used to predict behavior in so-called non-cooperative games – that is, games in which the players operate independently and do not form groups (coalitions) who make coordinated decisions. In the 1950s and 1960s, game theory languished at the margins of economics. Von Neumann and Morgenstern's *Theory of Games and Economic Behavior*, which many regard as the beginning of game theory, was published at Princeton during World War II and was immediately recognized as an enormous intellectual achievement. Nonetheless, for half a century the study of game theory barely extended beyond the mathematics and operations research departments. Only in the 1970s did game theory penetrate into the core of economics. If till then a market and competitive equilibrium constituted the major tool of economic analysis, they were now joined by the related duo of a games and Nash equilibrium. Since the 1980s, countless people have delighted in declaring that game theory is useful in all fields: competition between few competitors and company takeovers in economics, strategic voting and negotiation between countries in political science, the relations between flowers and butterflies and the evolution of animals in biology, moral issues in philosophy, developing communication protocols in computer science, and even the biblical stories of the binding of Isaac and the judgment of Solomon – all have been examined with the tools of game theory.

Game theory won media acclaim in 1994 thanks to "the mother of all auctions": some $7 billion in communications frequencies were sold by the Federal Communications Commission (FCC) in a public auction planned in consultation with game theorists. The bidders in the tender also hired game theory experts to advise them. In the media, and not only there, this event was seen as definitive proof of the applicability of game theory. I have my doubts.

I personally know some of the people who planned this tender and similar tenders. They are undoubtedly bright and intelligent. They are also people with two feet firmly on the ground. However, to the best of my understanding, they based their recommendations on basic intuitions and human simulations, and not on sophisticated models of game theory. I do not find any basis for claiming that it was game theory that helped them in planning the tender. At most, these advisors were intimately familiar with a specific type of strategic considerations that we often study in game theory.

During the years that game theory flourished, John Nash was diagnosed as a paranoid schizophrenic. He was hospitalized a number of times in mental hospitals, received insulin treatments, heard voices that crowned him "King of Antarctica," and communicated with other worlds via the pages of *The New York Times*.

November 1994

I sat in my office at Princeton. It was evening, the door was open. John Nash walked by in the hallway and seemed to be looking for something. He entered my room and asked politely whether I knew the fax number of someone at Stockholm University. The number he had was a six-digit number and since all telephone and fax numbers in the U.S. have seven digits, Nash figured that there was a digit missing in the number he had. Based on what I knew, I explained to him that in Stockholm the telephone and fax numbers have six digits (as they did at the time). He felt relieved. I exploited the moment to do something that I had wanted to do for quite a while and had not dared. I mustered the courage and handed him a copy of a text book about game theory that I had written together with Martin Osborne. Nash took the book. I do not remember him thanking me. He mentioned that he already had two books on game theory on his shelf and now he would have "two plus one = three books." And then, leafing through the book, he said in surprise: "I see that my name appears here."

Usefulness

Is game theory useful? The popular literature is full of nonsense about the applications of game theory. Here is an example from a serious newspaper, the *Financial Times* (17 April 2002):

> Kofi Annan is famously active in seeking advice from a variety of sources, and recent propositions from the United Nations' secretary general suggest he has found a new font of inspiration as he casts about for tips on how to solve the seemingly intractable crisis in the Middle East: game theory. Even Mr Annan's language has taken a turn for the mathematical. In several of his most recent speeches, the career bureaucrat has called on the US to help Israel and the Palestinians abandon their 'logic of war' for a 'logic of peace.'

And here is another example: February 2006 was a tense month in Thailand. The opposition demanded the prime minister's resignation. Seven months later, the pressure culminated in a military coup. During the same month, I happened to be in Bangkok and delivered one of the public lectures about game theory that I mentioned earlier. I emphasized my opinion that game theory is not relevant to practical questions. Of course, I did not make any reference to the political situation in Thailand. The closest I came to making a reference to Thailand was when I complimented the audience for being particularly generous in the Ultimatum Game. That was sufficient for a reporter from the Thai newspaper *The Nation*, who attended the lecture and wrote about it the following day, to lead with a headline: "Time to go to the polls, game theory says."

There is disagreement in the game theory community regarding the applicability of the theory. Some believe that the function of game theory is to provide useful predictions of behavior in strategic situations. The economist Hal Varian wrote in a review of the film *A Beautiful Mind*:

"Mr. Nash's contribution was far more important than the somewhat contrived analysis about whether or not to approach the beautiful woman in the bar. What he discovered was a way to predict the outcome of virtually any kind of strategic interaction" (*The New York Times*, 11 April 2002). We will get to the beautiful woman at the bar later, but I have absolutely no idea how Varian reached the conclusion about the predictive ability of Nash equilibrium. Even when a game has a single equilibrium, there remains a huge disparity between the prediction of game theory and reality. In addition, in many games there are multiple Nash equilibria and this narrows their potential to predict. And this is before noting the fundamental difficulty of predicting the behavior of individuals when they are exposed to a prediction and are likely to respond to it. Incidentally, the article (published in the journal *Econometrica* in 1951) for which Nash was awarded the Nobel Prize is devoid of any pretension of usefulness in economics. The only "economic" example you will find there is a simplification of a poker game with three players.

Economists such as Avinash Dixit and Barry Nalebuff believe in the power of game theory to enhance strategic intelligence. The study of game theory is supposed somehow to foster the ability to play in strategic situations. But even they do not regard game theory as a collection of guidelines on "how to...".

Game theory rhetoric switches between usefulness on the one hand, and awareness that it is dealing with simplified models, on the other. All in all, it seems to me that game theory tends to present a false front of usefulness. The Thai journalist evidently heard in my remarks what he wanted to hear. Nonetheless, I do not believe that he would write such a headline if I were a physicist or mathematician. Something in the language we use in economics and game theory creates an illusion that we understand and leads to the hasty application of ideas.

My view of game theory is consistent with my approach to economic models in general, as explained in Chapter 0. Game theory does not try to describe reality or be normative. Game theory investigates the logic of strategic thinking. But just as logic does not make people truthful or guide judges to just decisions, game theory does not assist players in playing games. If game theory has a practical aspect, it is derived indirectly. It enables us to conduct an orderly discussion of the concept of rationality in interactive situations. It enriches the discussion of economics and other fields of social sciences by focusing on strategic considerations, some of which we might not have been aware of. It is entertaining. And that is something; but it is not what people generally describe as useful. Incidentally, sometimes I wonder why we need to address the question of the usefulness of game theory at all. Does academic research have to be judged according to the immediate and practical benefit it brings?

Despite my reservations about the predictive ability of game theory, I do not deny the fact that people's behavior in game situations follows certain rules or patterns, which can be discovered by observing events in the world or by experimental results. But it is connected only loosely (if at all) to game theory analysis. Here is another example:

A treasure hunt

Treasure Hunt was my favorite radio program during my childhood. The program was broadcast once every four weeks at 9 pm. The theme music sounded as if it came straight from the courts of medieval knights. The treasure hunter in the studio would receive the riddle and turn to the audience with questions, and the listeners would call the studio and offer their answers for a price. If the treasure hunter identified the location of the treasure and his emissary reached the treasure before 10:20 pm, he would receive 1,000 lira, minus the payments he made to listeners. I would collect in advance all of my Land of Israel books and would concoct innovative solutions to infiltrate the busy phone lines. My excitement reached a peak during the few occasions when the treasure hunter purchased the answer of "a schoolboy from Jerusalem" for 5 lira. When I think of examples for the game theory course, my thoughts wander to *Treasure Hunt*. This radio program was also the inspiration for the following game that appears on the book's website:

> You have a treasure that you can hide in one of four boxes that are set up in a line and marked as follows:

> A   B   A   A

> Your competitor will have an opportunity to open only one box. Your goal is for the competitor not to find the treasure.

> In which box will you hide the treasure?

This situation can be thought of as a game with two players – the hider and the seeker. The hider has four strategies, one for each box in which he can hide the treasure. The seeker has four strategies, one for each box in which the treasure may be hidden. A pair of choices by the hider and the seeker leads to one of two possible outcomes: the seeker finds the treasure or the seeker does not find the treasure. The seeker prefers the first outcome and the hider the second.

There is an absolute conflict of interests between the two players in this game. The hider wants to reduce the probability of the seeker finding the treasure. The seeker seeks to increase the probability of finding the treasure. Anything that is good for one player is necessarily bad for the other player. In professional jargon, it is customary to call this type of game a zero-sum game. Public figures and columnists frequently use this concept, appropriately or inappropriately, in order to embellish their remarks with learned terms.

In this game, a candidate for Nash equilibrium is a pair of choices: the box in which the hider places the treasure and the box the seeker opens. If the two choices are identical, the seeker finds the treasure, and thus the hider would have done better to place the treasure in a different box. If the two choices are not identical, the treasure will not be found, and thus the seeker would have done better to open a different box. Therefore, this game does not have a Nash equilibrium.

The situation is different when the description of the game includes the possibility that a player chooses a box randomly. According to this approach, the hider chooses four non-negative numbers that must add up to 1. In the professional jargon, we call this type of choice a mixed strategy. Each number corresponds to the probability of the treasure being placed in one of the boxes. For example, the choice of (0.3, 0.2, 0.2, 0.3) means that there is a probability of 30% that he will hide the treasure in each of the two outermost boxes and a 20% probability for each of the two innermost boxes. Or, the choice of (1, 0, 0, 0) means that the hider definitely places the treasure in the left-most box. Similarly, for the seeker, a mixed strategy is a choice of four non-negative numbers that add up to 1, with each number corresponding to the probability that he will open a particular box.

Each player can be regarded as someone who spins a roulette wheel with four slots. Each slot in the roulette table corresponds to one of the boxes and its relative area corresponds to the probability that the player chooses the respective box. The result of the spin of the roulette wheel determines which box the player will choose. We do not necessarily think of the player as someone who actually spins the wheel. The randomness can be a result of a process that occurs inside the mind of the player when he decides to choose one of the four boxes. And, for someone looking on from the side, it may seem that the player uses a random method to choose the particular box.

A pair of mixed strategies defines the probability that the treasure will be found. For example, if the hider places the treasure in the four boxes (A, B, A, A) with the probabilities (0.3, 0.2, 0.2, 0.3) and the seeker opens the boxes with the probabilities of (0.1, 0.4, 0.4, 0.1), the seeker will have a 22% probability of finding the treasure. There is a probability of 30% that the treasure will be hidden in the left-most box and a probability of 10% that the seeker will open this box. Consequently, there is a probability of 3% that treasure will be hidden in the left-most box and that the seeker will also open this box. Similarly, there is an 8% probability that the treasure will be hidden and found in the box marked "B", and so on.

A candidate for Nash equilibrium is a pair of mixed strategies, one for the hider and one for the seeker. In order for the pair of strategies to be an equilibrium, neither of the players benefits by switching his strategy to another strategy. That is, when the hider is aware of the seeker's strategy, the hider does not have an alternative strategy that reduces the probability that the treasure is found; and when the seeker is aware of the hider's strategy, the seeker does not have an alternative strategy that increases the probability of finding the treasure.

Each of the following two reasons is sufficient to determine that the aforementioned pair of strategies is not an equilibrium: (i) The seeker's strategy is to open the boxes with probabilities (0.1, 0.4, 0.4, 0.1). The hider can reduce the probability that the treasure will be found from 22% to 10% if he places the treasure in one of the outermost boxes with a probability of 1. (ii) The hider places the treasure in boxes with probabilities (0.3, 0.2, 0.2, 0.3). The seeker can increase the probability of finding the treasure from 22% to 30% if he searches for the treasure in one of the outermost boxes.

It is possible to confirm that in the game's only equilibrium each of the players chooses each box with a probability of ¼ and, therefore, the probability of finding the treasure is ¼.

Of course, one can also think of the Treasure Hunt Game in ways other than Nash equilibrium. Here is one alternative. Let's say that you are participating in the game in the role of the hider. You are a pessimistic person and believe that whichever mixed strategy you choose the other player will correctly guess this strategy and then choose the best action for him (and therefore the worst from your perspective). If you choose a mixed strategy in which all of the probabilities are not equal, then there is at least one box in which you could hide the treasure with a probability greater than ¼. The pessimistic approach leads you to think that the seeker will surely open this box and, therefore, the treasure will be found with a probability of more than ¼. On the other hand, if you hide the treasure with a probability of ¼ in each of the four boxes, you will ensure that the seeker finds the treasure with a probability of only ¼. Consequently, in light of the pessimistic expectations regarding your competitor's moves, you would hide the treasure with equal probabilities in each of the boxes. In game theory, we call this type of strategy a max-min strategy.

Similarly, we can see that the seeker's max-min strategy is to search for the treasure at equal probabilities in each of the four boxes. Thus, we found that in the Treasure Hunt Game the equilibrium strategies and the max-min strategies are identical. This is no coincidence. We noted that the game is a zero-sum game: Whatever is good for me is bad for the other player, and vice versa. A central result in game theory, called the max-min theorem, teaches us that in every zero-sum game (and not only in the Treasure Hunt Game), Nash equilibrium strategies are identical to max-min strategies. In this way, it becomes clear that the two ways of looking at the game, which appear to be so disparate at first glance, lead to identical conclusions in games with absolute conflicts of interest. This is game theory at its best.

Let's return to the Treasure Hunt Game. Imagine for a moment that you are the seeker. If you believe in the predictions of game theory, you are not particularly anxious, because you know that the treasure is hidden with equal probabilities in each of the boxes. Therefore, it makes no difference to you which box is opened. But in light of the survey results of 5,500 hiders, I hope for your sake that you will indeed devote some attention to your choice. The distribution of the choice of boxes (A, B, A, A) is: (19%, 25%, 34%, 22%). The middle box marked "A" is the most popular choice in nearly every group of students participating in the survey. (I have no idea why the box marked "B" was the most popular choice in one very large group, at Tilburg University in Holland.) If these data predict the behavior of the hider you are competing against, then if you choose the middle box marked A, your chances of finding the treasure will increase to 34%.

In another survey, 3,500 students were randomly assigned to be hiders or seekers. Among the hiders, the distribution of choice was strikingly similar to the large sample population (17%, 25%, 35%, 23%). Among the seekers, the results were even more dramatic (11%, 27%, 47%, 15%). This result leads me to think that if I had hidden the treasure I would have placed it in the left-most box and had a 89% chance of keeping it for myself, which is much higher than the game theory prediction of only 75% probability of success in hiding the treasure from the seeker.

So here is a "useful" finding. Let's say that I was a strategic advisor to the U.S. Army in its efforts to wipe out Saddam Hussein in 2003, and let's assume that there were four palaces in Baghdad arranged along the Tigris River like the four boxes in the diagram, that one of them (marked with the letter "B") was the most prominent palace, and that it was possible to bomb only one palace.

If I had assumed that they had not read the results of this study in Baghdad, then I would have recommended attacking the central palace marked A.

If I had thought that Saddam Hussein's advisors had read the results of this study and had assumed that the U.S. Army was unaware of the study, I would have concluded that his advisors would recommend to him that he hide in one of the outermost palaces and I would have recommended to the Americans that they attack one of them.

And if it was well known that they had read about the study in both Washington and Baghdad – I would have had no idea what to advise.

In any case, even if this finding is useful, and can be used for good or bad (depending on which side uses it), it is totally unrelated to an analysis of the game with the tools of game theory.

1998

For years, I believed that teaching game theory is not helpful and is even harmful because it can potentially encourage selfishness and deviousness. In 1998, a wonderful group of students gathered at Tel Aviv University for a seminar on economic theory. Most of the participants were pursuing academic studies as part of their military service and, because they appeared in uniform, the seminar was nicknamed "the officers' seminar." I proposed to them that they tackle the mission of proving that the teaching of game theory is harmful. We composed a questionnaire that included a series of imaginary decision problems. It seemed to us that certain decisions express a tendency toward egoistic and manipulative behavior. We asked students who were about to start a game theory course, as well as other students who had already completed the course, to respond to the questionnaire. We expected that a comparison of the responses by the two groups would show that studying game theory at the undergraduate level makes the students more selfish and devious. But nothing of the sort happened. We did not find any effect of game theory on anything. But I still believe such an effect exists.

A Beautiful Mind

Dozens of journalists wrote about Nash's winning of the Nobel Prize in Economics in 1994. Everyone applauded game theory. Sylvia Nasar was the only one who recognized that the announcement of the prize was more than just a triumph for game theory – it was an event with a strong human touch. She published an article that stretched over two full pages in *The New York Times*, describing Nash in three stages: a young and handsome genius; a sick person roaming the idyllic campus of Princeton like a ghost; and finally, the happy ending: Nash recuperates, returns to activity and wins the Nobel Prize. The article touched people's hearts and led to the writing of the book in which Nasar delved into the depths of Nash's mind and delusions. The book's success led to its being made into a film. From the public perspective, the book and film focused the attention of millions of people on mental illness and the discrimination against those who suffer from it, and instilled new hope in patients and their families.

There are a number of inaccuracies in the film. For example, after Nash is notified that he has been awarded the Nobel Prize, there is an impressive scene: a ceremony of academic deference in which we see Nash sitting in the coffee room of Fine Hall and one professor after another comes up to him and places a pen on the table (you can watch this scene on this book's website: http://www.openbookpublishers.com/exsites/136). I happened to be there.

11 October 1994

In the morning, the announcement was made that John Harsanyi, Reinhard Selten and Nash would jointly receive the Nobel Prize "for their pioneering analysis of equilibria in the theory of non-cooperative games."

Princeton University reacted to the announcement with embarrassment. Nash had no formal affiliation with the university at the time. Only out of kindness had the university provided him with a computer account. Nash was umbilically connected to the Mathematics Department at Princeton and resided in the town of Princeton, which was also the home of most of the people in the world who cared about him. How do you explain to the world that the Nobel Prize recipient is from Princeton, but not from Princeton University? In consultation with the governors of the university, the Mathematics Department decided to arrange a modest celebratory gathering to toast Nash's award. In the department's tea room, a number of math professors gathered, along with students who happened to be there and a very small number of economics professors. The senior university officials were there and perhaps a photographer too. The beginning of the ceremony was delayed for reasons that were unclear. Glasses were raised, and a few very brief congratulatory remarks were made. The guest of honor maintained the right to remain silent. When the participants finished their drinks, a general uneasiness spread over the room. Nash stood alone in the center of the room. No one approached him. He walked toward the table of refreshments and said to me and others who stood near the table: "The cookies today are better than they usually are." To the best of my knowledge, there was and is no pen ceremony anywhere. No such ceremony even took place metaphorically. Nash received an office from the university and an ID card that enabled him to enter Princeton's faculty club. But no one addressed Nash as "master" as in the film.

The bar scene

What happens when Hollywood tries to explain game theory? In one scene in the movie (which, again, you can view on the book's website: http://www.openbookpublishers.com/exsites/136), a group of students, including the young Nash, enter a pickup bar. Which girl to approach? The proud, stunning blonde who will only react to you if no one else approaches her, or one of the many unexceptional brunettes at the bar with whom your chances are much higher? You do not need to have experience in bars to realize that there is a place here for strategic thinking. The rational courtier will choose his objective in line with his expectations of his friends' behavior.

We will simplify the story and assume that Nash goes to the bar with only one friend (although in the movie, there are four men in the group). Each contemplates whether to pursue the striking blonde or turn his attention to one of the many brunettes in the bar. In keeping with the film, we will assume that if both men pursue the blonde, she will turn her back on both of them and they will end up alone that evening. If only one of them pursues the blonde, he will win her coveted company while his friend will have to settle for one of the less desirable brunettes. If both of them refrain from approaching the blonde, both of them will be able to spend the evening with a brunette.

We can present the story in the following table:

The outcome if...

and the other man chooses

	Blonde	Brunette
Blonde	lonely	gets the blonde
Brunette	gets the brunette and envies...	gets the brunette

a man chooses

One player controls the choice of row and a second player the choice of column. Each square contains a description of the result from the perspective of the player who chooses the row. For example, if the row player chooses to pursue the blonde and the column player turns to the brunette, the result from the perspective of the row player is winning the blonde.

This description brings us closer to presenting the situation in the conventional language of game theory. In each square, we insert a number that represents the amount of utility the player derives from the result described in the square. If the number assigned to one square is higher than the number assigned to another square, this means that the player prefers the result in the former to the result in the latter.

	Blonde	Brunette
Blonde	0	4
Brunette	1	2

The highest number was assigned to the result in which the row player wins the blonde's company. The lowest number was assigned to remaining alone. In the middle are the two possibilities in which the row player finds consolation in the arms of a brunette. His consolation will be greater if the other player does not find a way to the blonde's heart.

In the game theory literature, this game is called **Chicken**. It has two Nash equilibria. In one equilibrium, Nash pursues the blonde and his friend suffices with the brunette. In the second equilibrium, Nash suffices with the brunette and his friend pursues the blonde.

Just for fun, I asked the audience at the lectures on "Game Theory and John Nash" to play the game. About 46% of some 3,000 men and 48% of about 1,500 women chose the blonde. The Dutch and the Israelis were the boldest: 56% of the men and women chose the blonde. Actually, I do not know whether this finding is an expression of strategic boldness in bars or simply differences in the preference of hair color.

The discussion of the game in the movie is confused and misleading. Nash in the movie says that he discovered a contradiction in a principle that has been accepted in economics since the time of Adam Smith:

> Adam Smith said the best outcome for the group comes from everybody trying to do what's best for himself. He was wrong. The best outcome comes from everybody trying to do what's best for himself and the group.

The message attributed to Smith in the film is simplistic. In what sense does each individual's concern for himself generate the best result? What is best for a group that includes individuals with disparate interests? In any case, the discovery attributed to Nash – who argued that if people act in a self-centered way the result for the group is actually liable to be worse than if people act in a socially responsible way – is not well demonstrated in the bar scene.

The idea is presented clearly in the game called the **Prisoner's Dilemma**, a game that has lost some of its luster after being used so often to illustrate game theory. The Prisoner's Dilemma involves two prisoners who are apprehended while committing a misdemeanor and are suspected of committing a serious crime. But the Prisoner's Dilemma Game can also be expressed as follows: there are a number of residents on a street, and the level of cleanliness in the street depends on whether or not the residents of the street keep it clean. Let's say that each resident believes that, regardless of what the neighbors do, his exertion in maintaining cleanliness is more bothersome to him than the marginal increase in environmental damage that would result if he discontinued this effort. At the same time, let's also assume that every resident would prefer a situation in which all residents maintained the cleanliness and the street remained clean, rather than having all residents, including himself, neglecting the cleanliness and living amidst the stench of garbage. Of course, each resident only controls his own actions.

This game does not require a player to enter the other's shoes. Whatever the player believes regarding the behavior of the other players, it would be best for him to not make an effort to preserve the cleanliness. Consequently, if all of the residents are rational, the sad result is that no one maintains the cleanliness and the street smells. Each player acts only to promote his own interests and the result is worse than if all of the residents maintain the street's cleanliness. To the best of my knowledge, the Prisoner's Dilemma Game was formulated by Albert Tucker, and he has no connection to Nash's contribution to game theory.

A beautiful mind

Nash is depicted in the movie as someone who managed to gain control of the delusional voices he heard, as someone who discovers the true meaning of life when he lovingly offers his wife a white kerchief, and as someone who returns to the academic world. If I were to choose an ending to the movie I would choose a different one, a bit more melancholy. In his autobiography, Nash noted that he also lost something during his recuperation process. He characterizes the period of irrationality as a time of " dream-like delusional hypotheses" and describes his return to "thinking rationally again in the style that is characteristic of scientists," as a process that "is not entirely a matter of joy" because rationality of thought "imposes a limit on a person's concept of his relations to the cosmos."

The story of Nash is the journey of his transformation from a descriptive term in an abstract mathematical concept into a human being. The title crazy genius is for us an invitation to an encounter with other worlds. We try to imagine the voices that Nash heard and ask where he was during the thirty years when he walked among us but was not with us. People who are different scare us, but we are also attracted to them. Curious and scared, we confront our prejudices and try to accept that someone who is mentally ill, even if he is different from us, deserves to be one of us.

As for me, I was fortunate to be present at stages of Nash's journey and the march of game theory from the margin of economics to its core. And what do I find in game theory? A beautiful mind. It is interesting because it touches upon the way we think about the world. It is beautiful because it offers lucid formulations for what appears to be confusing. It has the same interest and beauty that I find in philosophy, mathematics, logic and literature. If in a circuitous way that I am unaware of it can also be useful – then so much the better. But, in my view, usefulness is neither the criterion nor the essence.

3. The Jungle Tale and the Market Tale

An exercise in rhetoric

This chapter summarizes the very first lectures in two Introductory Economics courses. One lecture is from the Introduction to the Jungle Economy course. This is a unique course that you cannot learn anywhere else. I will ask you to imagine that you are listening to it in the straw huts of Lubungulu University, located deep in the thick, dark, green jungle. The purpose of this lecture is to present the basic idea of the jungle economy. The second lecture launches the Introduction to the Market Economy course. There is no need to travel to a far-off, exotic venue in order to attend this course. It is a course that anyone can take as part of the curriculum in the nearest Department of Economics, assuming, of course, that he is accepted into this prestigious club. Many people cram for this course, believing that it is essential for reaching the top. Some regard it as a guide to the economic galaxies – the nearby galaxy where we live, and the distant galaxy, where they would like us to live. The goal of this lecture is to present the basic idea of the market economy.

In both of these lectures, I will follow economic tradition and demonstrate the ideas via models – tales or fables. I will try to present the models precisely, with each claim accompanied by a real proof. But I will not use formal language, which would indeed make the models easier to understand for the few who are familiar with this language, but would pose an impenetrable barrier for all the rest.

Throughout this chapter, we will skip back and forth between the two lectures: jungle, market, jungle, market, and so on. You can consult two means of illustration – one for the jungle model and one for the market model – that are posted on the book's website. When we are done, you will be asked a somewhat banal question: what are the similarities and differences between the two?

First lesson in the introduction to jungle economics course

Ladies and gentlemen, distinguished students, welcome to the first lecture in the Introduction to Jungle Economics course. In this lecture, we will study the principles of the economic system practiced in our society. We will see how an **iron hand** – not an invisible one – leads to an efficient result without the need for government intervention.

You know that you have come to the most popular course at the Lubungulu Jungle University. All of you passed the JAT (Jungle Aptitude Test) before being accepted to the class. You all excelled in marksmanship and pushups. But the truth is that the principles we will discuss are simple, and the abilities you have demonstrated are not essential for understanding the course material. Take a good look at the man on your right, and then on your left; because next year both of them will be here as well.

What is economics? I do not pose this question because it is important for me to put something into your heads that is not there, but rather to remove something that already is there. I assume that you have drawn your impressions about the field of economics primarily from the economics sections of the daily newspapers. However, academic economics does not deal with boring tables and gossip you are accustomed to calling economics. Our main task is to study the social mechanisms that determine what goods are available to us and that allocate them among individuals. If you hope the course will help you succeed in the complex environment of the jungle, I am afraid you are in for a disappointment. We, the teachers at the Jungle University, do not engage in professional training. We place the practical matters in the trusty hands of our brave military heroes. I am convinced that you jungle cadets will know how to conduct your lives successfully thanks to your common sense. You have come this far because you and your forefathers survived the hardships of the world. There is no useful advice that I, whose attention is entirely devoted to academic issues, can offer you. The aim of the courses in our research university is purely and simply to satisfy your curiosity, to enrich your language and to introduce you to new, unfamiliar ways of thinking.

Common interests and conflicts of interests intermingle in the jungle experience. There are things we can achieve only through collaboration: nearly every act of production requires a series of coordinated activities conducted by many people. It is vital for all of us to mobilize for defend and conquer missions. Nonetheless, the resources available to any society, even a flourishing society like ours, are limited. Everyone seeks to receive as much as possible of what he likes. And, often, what one person likes others also like.

In our view, economics is no more than a tool that helps us to achieve common objectives and to overcome conflicts of interests. Our economic perspective is part of our broader social and political outlook. We are aware of the fact that some countries try to separate economics and politics. Economic questions that ought to be decided democratically via the political system are treated there as if they were professional matters and are deferred to experts to decide. We believe this is a ploy that serves the stronger members of society (including, just by chance, the community of experts). In this course, we will see that our economic system brings order to the chaos, leads to an effective allocation of what we have, and enables us to realize our aspirations for territorial expansion.

There are no invisible hands in the jungle. Everything is clear and simple. Our economic system was designed based on an understanding of human nature. We are aware of the aggression inherent in each of us. We are not ashamed to admit that we believe in anarchist philosophies. Actually, our cultural heroes are anarchist philosophers. Our slogans are: "We owe each other nothing" and "Men merely use each other as tools." Our flourishing and prosperous jungle culture does not suppress man's drives. We encourage aggression and harness it for the just and eternal struggle of the tribe against the enemies who rise up against us and seek to annihilate us. We also know how to channel these aggressive impulses to lubricate the wheels of the social and economic order. And if you become faint-hearted and start having doubts about our use of the aggressive instinct, remember that you cannot argue with success. Just look at the prosperity our economic system has brought us.

In the lecture today, we will see that recognizing that each individual should grab what he can with "a strong hand and an outstretched arm" brings about an efficient outcome, prevents (or at least reduces) the need for wasteful and corrupt government intervention and frees us of the central planning mechanisms that have failed time and again throughout human history.

In the best economic tradition, we will understand the economic mechanism of the jungle via a model, which we will affectionately call the jungle tale.

First lesson in the introduction to market economics course

Ladies and gentlemen, distinguished students, welcome to the first lecture in the Introduction to Market Economics course. In this lecture we will study the principles of the market economy. We will see how an **invisible hand** leads to an efficient result in a competitive environment, without the need for government intervention.

I salute you for being accepted into the economics program, the most popular in our university. You are here thanks to your wonderful achievements in the SAT (Scholastic Assessment Test), which predicts – among other things – your ability to succeed in multiple-choice tests, a skill that is essential for the final exam in the course. The Introduction to Market Economics (or Principles as it is commonly named) is a challenging course. As Paul Samuelson used to say: "Take a good look at the man on your right, and then on your left; because next year one of you won't be here."

We cannot start the lecture without first saying something about the question, what is economics? Economics deals with individuals' and society's decision making processes. It examines how people make decisions. For example, should we send our son to university or buy him a car? Should we develop the health system or build highways? Should we enjoy more leisure time or try to increase our earnings? Economics helps us to best exploit our limited resources. It enables us to anticipate the changes engendered by government measures or environmental change. Economics has something to say about almost every issue, public or private. Economics will help us to conduct our lives rationally.

We act with the awareness that in our society there are common interests as well as conflicts of interests. In order to realize the aspirations of prosperity and growth, we all need to work vigorously and harmoniously to increase production. However, the resources available to any society, even a prosperous society like ours, are limited; and everyone wants to receive more and work less. The market economy is designed to promote common interests and deal with conflicting ones.

Our economic system is based on an understanding of human nature. We, in the advanced world, are aware of the selfishness inherent in each of us and harness it to the achievement of economic prosperity. Our system channels individuals' desire for wealth so that it serves as the fuel that powers the economic order. As Adam Smith said: "Every individual ... [is] led by an invisible hand to promote an end which was no part of his intention. Nor is it always the worse for the society that it was no part of it. By pursuing his own interest he frequently promotes that of the society more effectually than when he really intends to promote it" (*The Wealth of Nations*, Book 4, Chapter 2).

In today's lecture, we will see how the realization that each individual should strive to obtain maximal wealth for himself without considering others results in an efficient outcome, prevents (or at least reduces) the need for wasteful and corrupt government intervention, and frees us of the mechanisms of central planning that have proved throughout history to be dangerous. The course also has practical objectives. After completing your studies, most of you will become economists, managers, merchants and bankers. Understanding the market mechanism will help you to succeed in whatever path you choose. The course will help you to think intelligently about economic questions that trouble the public. How unfortunate it is that economic affairs are left in the hands of populist politicians and not in the hands of professional economists capable of implementing what the course teaches and putting the world to rights.

In the best of economic tradition, we will present the economic mechanism of the market via a model which we will call the market model.

The jungle tale

The territory controlled by our tribe is divided into a number of homesteads, inhabited by our notables, the heroic warriors whose courage enabled us to conquer our homeland. The number of heroes is equal to the number of homesteads. Each homestead can accommodate one hero, and each hero occupies only one homestead. The homesteads differ from each other. Each hero ranks the homesteads according to his own individual preferences. One might think that the conflict of interests between the heroes would generate chaos: a number of heroes might claim the same homestead, arguing "I deserve it" or "I was here first" or "God promised me this homestead" or "my ancestors were here 3,000 years ago." In this lecture, we will see how the laws of the jungle allocate homesteads among the heroes.

Let's say that the tribe has six homesteads. One of them has **oil** and one includes a **beach**. One has **a vineyard** and there is a thick **forest** in another. The **tomb** of King Gulu I is located in one distant homestead and the big city homestead incorporates the famous **nightclub** Desire. The six heroes, A, B,

C, D, E, F, will settle in the homesteads. In the table below, each column shows one hero's ranking of the homesteads (in declining order). In a moment, we will explain the meaning of the number that appears in the table under each hero. At this stage, you can ignore the asterisks.

The Jungle Model

Hero	A	B	C	D	E	F
Strength	55	50	45	40	35	30
Ranking						
1	Vineyard*	Vineyard	Oil*	Beach	Beach	Nightclub*
2	Oil	Beach*	Forest	Oil	Vineyard	Oil
3	Nightclub	Oil	Vineyard	Forest*	Oil	Tomb
4	Beach	Forest	Beach	Nightclub	Tomb*	Vineyard
5	Tomb	Nightclub	Nightclub	Vineyard	Forest	Forest
6	Forest	Tomb	Tomb	Tomb	Nightclub	Beach

It is impossible to satisfy the wishes of all of the heroes. Two of them put the Vineyard homestead at the top of the list, and two have set their sights on the Beach homestead, but there is only one Vineyard homestead and only one Beach homestead. It is true that C snorts oil fumes, while A only ranks the Oil homestead in second place. But if A receives the oil fields, perhaps this will resolve the well-known centuries-old conflict between A and B over the wine country and bring peace to the residents of the jungle.

A mechanism is needed to allocate the homesteads and we can envisage many such mechanisms. One mechanism is the lottery. The homesteads are raffled between the heroes. They might grumble about the result of the lottery, but they cannot change it, even by consent. This mechanism is known to us from biblical times: "Notwithstanding the land shall be divided by lot; according to the names of the tribes of their fathers they shall inherit. According to the lot shall their inheritance be divided between the more and the fewer" (Numbers 26:55–56). When Joshua conducts this lottery in the biblical tale, God was also in the picture. But we'll disregard this fine detail. In any case, here in the jungle, we cannot accept the idea that a toss of the coin will determine who wins the land flowing with milk and honey, and who gets stuck with the desert wasteland. Here, we have a Basic Law of Good Reasons: every public decision must be predicated on appropriate and well-formulated reasons. The casting of lots is not listed in the Book of Good Reasons and Joshua's mechanism would not meet the criteria of the Supreme Court. Moreover, there are likely to be many dissatisfied individuals after the lottery who would be happy to engage in "swaps" between them if they could. Just imagine if the one who is allocated the Beach homestead cannot swim and the one who gets the Forest homestead is afraid of bears.

Another mechanism is an organizing committee. The elders of the tribe sit in the center of the village and members of the tribe come before them, one after the other, and report on their needs and aspirations. The honorable elders search (perhaps via the biological supercomputer we invented recently) for the best match of individuals and homesteads, for the glory of the tribe and to fulfill the vision of the prophets of efficiency. But here in the jungle we have little enthusiasm for organizing committees. We know that each committee of this type will turn us all into cheats and will corrupt our elders. And we believe not only in the Covenant of Thugs, but also in the values of the Movement for Quality Government.

And now we come to the mechanism that drives our prosperous economy. The allocation of homesteads in our society is dictated by the relative strength of the heroes. The balance of strength between any pair of heroes is defined unequivocally: either the first is stronger than the second, or the second is stronger than the first. In addition, we assume that if one hero is stronger than a second hero, and the second hero is stronger than a third hero, then the first hero is necessarily stronger than the third. In the table, the numbers assigned to the heroes are the strength indices. The numbers themselves have no significance beyond the fact that the higher the number, the stronger the hero.

The strength ranking of the heroes is known to all the jungle residents. All of the heroes are prepared to make unbridled use of their strength. The fact that one hero is stronger than a second hero means just one thing: the stronger one can grab any homestead held by the weaker one. There are no ownership contracts in the jungle. A hero can hold a homestead, but has no rights protecting him against someone who wants it. In our economy, unlike in a market economy, an exchange does not require a meeting of interests. One person, with one strong wish, is sufficient for a homestead to change hands. When a hero wants the homestead of someone who is weaker than him, he approaches him, greets him politely, and the two confirm their relative strength. In the worst case, they exchange a number of polite blows and the weaker one leaves the place submissively. Our inspiration for acting this way comes from nature – after all, we are part of it. In nature, it is enough for the stronger animal to remind the weaker one of the balance of strength between them to make the weaker one leave the nest or abandon the prey it is holding.

In our tale, as in a real jungle, the heroes cannot forge alliances to fight shoulder to shoulder for the interests of the members of the alliance. In the absence of a legal option to sign binding agreements, they find it impossible to organize into groups, even though they realize that they would benefit from forming such a coalition. In addition, we also have an antitrust law that prohibits individuals from organizing with the aim of exercising force against other heroes.

Like any tale, the jungle tale does not describe reality exactly as it is, but it simplifies what is complex and omits certain factors so that we can understand the operating principles of the jungle economy. In the tale, for example, the balance of strength decides every conflict between two heroes: in attack, the strong hero banishes the weaker hero from his homestead; and in defense, he prevents the weaker hero from expelling him from his home. In real life, on the other hand, things are a bit more complex. There is uncertainty, and sometimes David strikes down Goliath...

Another realistic factor that is not included in the model is that each evacuation of a homestead entails costs for both the one who is evicted and the one who expels him. These costs sometimes prevent a strong hero from exploiting his advantage over a weaker one. Some of the costs are real, such as removal costs. In addition, sometimes the weaker hero makes an error in judgment and rejects the demand of the stronger one and in the ensuing conflict the stronger one also pays a price and makes sacrifices. Some of the costs are mental ones: our warrior heroes are all sensitive souls, who experience profound discomfort when they are compelled to expel someone weak from the homestead he occupies.

In summary, the jungle tale begins with a presentation of the heroes and the homesteads, a description of the strength ranking and a list of each hero's preferences regarding the homesteads.

The market tale

The territory controlled by our society is divided into homesteads. A number of traders operate in the market, and each one owns a different homestead. There is no ownerless homestead. The ownership of a homestead cannot be divided among several traders, and each trader can own only one homestead. The homesteads differ from each other and each trader ranks the homesteads in a way that reflects his own preferences.

Let's say there are six homesteads in the market and six traders. In the following table, each column represents a trader. The homestead he owns at the beginning of trading appears at the top of the column, with his homestead rankings listed below it – in declining order. At this stage, you can disregard the asterisks and the row of prices.

The Market Model

Trader	A	B	C	D	E	F
Ownership	Beach	Oil	Tomb	Vineyard	Nightclub	Forest
Price	25	21	10	25	10	10
Ranking						
1	Vineyard*	Vineyard	Oil	Beach*	Beach	Nightclub*
2	Oil	Beach	Forest*	Oil	Vineyard	Oil
3	Nightclub	Oil*	Vineyard	Forest	Oil	Tomb
4	Beach	Forest	Beach	Nightclub	Tomb*	Vineyard
5	Tomb	Nightclub	Nightclub	Vineyard	Forest	Forest
6	Forest	Tomb	Tomb	Tomb	Nightclub	Beach

One might think that the process of allocating the homesteads is very chaotic, with several traders descending upon one trader and demanding that he swaps with them, making such claims as: "I deserve it," or "I have more to offer you," or "I came to you first," or "I'm the man, and if you don't comply with my demand I'll kick you out." In this lecture, we will see how the market mechanism imposes order on trading and leads to a stable and efficient allocation of homesteads.

Our economy sanctifies the concept of ownership. Owning a homestead means that no one is allowed to take the homestead from the owner against his will. This is not a jungle! A strong desire on one side is not sufficient for an exchange to be transacted. Each transaction requires a meeting of interests between two traders. Mankind has come a long way from the laws of the jungle to laws of ownership and contracts. The first commandment in our constitution is that no one has the right to impose anything on another person, and certainly no one is allowed to take something from someone else by force. Everything is conducted politely even though each trader is closely accompanied by an attorney. Each person is free to do what he wants… within the framework of budget constraints, of course.

We are aware that the concept of ownership in our model is simplistic. Sometimes there are disputes over ownership, resulting in violence between the rivals. Our legal system is designed to prevent situations in which two people try to occupy the same homestead, with each person insisting "It's mine."

In our model, the traders act as individuals. They are not allowed to form themselves into a group that coordinates the activity of its members in the market in order to obtain better assets. Such unions are also prohibited in real life by antitrust laws – laws that we enforce… sometimes.

The model ignores the existence of transaction costs. These include real costs – legal expenses and the costs of moving from one homestead to another; and mental costs – the traders are sensitive people and the heart of a trader cringes when he takes part in a deal that greatly improves his own situation but leaves his counterpart with only a small return. An expansion of the model to take into account the transaction costs would take us beyond the scope of this introductory lecture.

In summary, the presentation of the market model begins with introducing the traders and homesteads, a listing of homestead ownership, and a ranking of each trader's homestead preferences.

Solution of the jungle tale

Every tale seeks an ending. The conclusion of the jungle tale must be an allocation – that is, a description of which hero holds which homestead. There are many possible allocations, with the number increasing rapidly as the number of heroes grows. When there are only six homesteads and six heroes in the jungle, there are 720 possible allocations. We are interested in possible endings in which the force that might generate instability is neutralized – that is, no hero has an interest in exploiting his strength against those who are weaker than him.

A trumpet blast and we will unveil the solution concept that guides us in selecting the tale's ending.

Definition: We say that an allocation of the homesteads to the heroes is a **jungle equilibrium** if no hero prefers a homestead held by a weaker hero. In other words, in an allocation that is not an equilibrium, there is a hero who has his eyes on a homestead that is held by a weaker hero and is therefore up for grabs for him.

In general, after we define an equilibrium concept in economics, we verify that the requirements included in the definition are not so severe as to preclude any ending to the tale. Here as well, we are interested in proving that regardless of the heroes' preferences and the balance of strength between them, the jungle tale has a jungle equilibrium. Claims of this type are called existence theorems. Advanced mathematical tools are sometimes used in proving these theorems, but in the model of the jungle we need only basic logical deductions.

Jungle Claim 1: For each beginning of the jungle tale, the tale has an ending that is a jungle equilibrium.

> **Proof**: We will prove the claim by constructing an algorithm that will always lead to a jungle equilibrium. The algorithm is no more than a tool for proving the claim. It is an imaginary process and does not purport to describe the jungle dynamics.
>
> We summon the heroes, one after another – from the strongest to the weakest. First, we enable the strongest to choose one out of all the homesteads. Then we call upon the second strongest hero and allow him to choose any homestead, except the one already chosen by the stronger hero. And we continue onward: at each stage, we call upon the next hero in the ranking of strength and let him choose from among the homesteads that were not selected in the earlier stages by the stronger contenders. Each hero chooses the homestead that he considers the best one for him among those still available.
>
> The allocation resulting from the application of this algorithm is necessarily a jungle equilibrium. Why? The algorithm allocates to each hero the homestead he considers the best of those that have not been taken by those stronger than him. In other words, the hero regards his homestead as preferable to any of the homesteads allocated via the algorithm to those who are weaker than him. Therefore, no hero has an interest in attacking a weaker hero. It is definitely possible that

there are homesteads that he would prefer to the one the algorithm allotted to him, but these are held by stronger heroes, so he cannot seize them.

Let's apply the algorithm in the proof to the example of the six homesteads. Hero A is called first and chooses **Vineyard**. Hero B is called next. He would have liked to take **Vineyard**, but this homestead is already held by A. Of the homesteads that remain after A's selection, Hero B chooses **Beach**. Hero C will take the homestead that he ranks highest, **Oil**, since it was not allocated in the first two stages. Hero D can choose one of the three homesteads that remain after the three stronger heroes took Vineyard, Beach and Oil, and he decides to settle for **Forest**. Hero E will take **Tomb** and the weakest hero, F, is left with only one "choice," **Nightclub**, the only homestead that was not taken by one of the others. Fortunately for him, this homestead happens to be his heart's desire. The allocation of the homesteads is marked by asterisks in the table in the jungle model.

Now we know that the jungle model always has at least one ending that can withstand the forces threatening to undermine its stability. But an additional danger threatens the solution concept: perhaps there are too many possible endings that comply with the definition of jungle equilibrium. This would make the solution concept uninteresting. But there is no need to worry: whatever the heroes' preferences and balance of strength might be, there is exactly one equilibrium. This equilibrium will depend, of course, on the balance of strength and how the heroes rank the homesteads.

Jungle Claim 2: For each beginning, the jungle tale has only one ending that is a jungle equilibrium.

> **Proof**: To prove that there is only one allocation that constitutes a jungle equilibrium, we will show that in this equilibrium each hero must hold the homestead allotted to him by the algorithm from the proof of Jungle Claim 1.
>
> First, we will demonstrate that this is true with respect to the strongest hero. According to the jungle equilibrium, this hero does not prefer a homestead held by any other hero to the one he owns. Hence, in equilibrium, of all of the homesteads in the jungle he necessarily holds the one that he prefers. This is also the homestead the algorithm allocates to him. In order to see that in equilibrium all the other heroes also hold the homesteads allocated to them by the algorithm, we will use the method called proof by induction.
>
> Inductive step: If, in equilibrium, each of the N strongest heroes holds the homestead the algorithm allocated to them, then this is also true for the (N+1)th hero in the hierarchy of strength.
>
> Proof of the argument by induction: Let's assume that in equilibrium each of the N strongest heroes holds the homestead the algorithm allocated to him. It follows that the homesteads that remain available after the algorithm has allotted N homesteads to the N strongest heroes are in equilibrium in the hands of the weaker ones. According to the definition of the jungle equilibrium, the (N+1)th hero prefers the homestead he possesses in equilibrium to all of the homesteads held by those weaker than him. Therefore, in equilibrium, of all the homesteads the algorithm did not allocate to the N strongest heroes, he holds the homestead he prefers, and it is precisely the homestead the algorithm has allocated to him. Since we have proven that, in equilibrium, the strongest hero holds the homestead

the algorithm has allotted to him, it follows by induction that this is true for the second hero, the third hero, and thus for all the heroes.

Let's summarize: the concept of the jungle equilibrium predicts a single ending for each jungle tale.

Solution of the market tale

Let's go back and look at the example of the six homesteads. There are many barter transactions that would improve on the starting positions of the traders. Which of these transactions will be executed? It is worthwhile for C and E to swap Tomb and Nightclub. Will they indeed do so? Will B, who owns the Oil homestead, trade it with E for Nightclub (despite the fact that Nightclub is less preferable to B than his current holding) because he plans to make a trade with D subsequently in which he will receive Nightclub, his greatest dream, in exchange for Vineyard? The traders D and E compete to obtain the Beach homestead owned by A. Trader D can offer A the Vineyard homestead and E can offer Nightclub. Will the fact that D has more to offer help him get the Beach?

The solution of the model of the market must describe who ultimately owns each homestead. We believe in a solution concept called competitive equilibrium, whose definition is based on the concept of **price**. A sign is posted next to each homestead. When the traders wake for a morning of commerce, they see on each sign a number called a price. The prices on the signs comprise a **price list**. It functions like a traffic sign. At some of the turnoffs

from the road, signs are posted that restrict the passage
of certain types of vehicles. Every driver knows that he is
allowed to turn only at an exit that does not have a sign
restricting entry to his vehicle. Of the permitted turnoffs,
he will choose the one that is best for him. Similarly, a
trader knows that he cannot obtain a homestead whose
price is higher than the price of his own, and he chooses
the one he most prefers from among the homesteads
within his price range.

Not every set of prices posted on signs will direct the
flow of commerce without collisions. It is very possible
that a certain homestead will be sought by more than one
trader. We are looking for a set of prices that will steer
commerce in such a way that each homestead will be the
right one for only one trader. The fateful hour has arrived.
The clamor of Wall Street can be heard in the background,
creating a festive atmosphere as the moment when we
announce the central concept of the lecture approaches.

Definition: A set of prices is called a **set of competitive
equilibrium prices** if it satisfies the following requirement:
for each homestead, there is exactly one trader who
regards it as the best among the homesteads whose price
is not higher than the price of the one he owns at the start
of trading. The allocation that results from the traders'
choices is called a **competitive equilibrium**.

In the table in the market tale section, one price list
is displayed. In each column in the table, an asterisk
marks the homestead the respective trader seeks to
purchase given the price list. Trader A can acquire any
homestead and he chooses Vineyard. Trader B would
like to acquire Beach and Vineyard, but their prices

are higher than that of his initial homestead. He has no alternative but to settle for the Oil homestead. Trader C, who owns the Tomb homestead, can only trade it for Forest or Nightclub, and the Forest homestead is higher in his preferences. Similarly, D would like the Beach, E wants the Tomb and F seeks Nightclub. Thus we find that for each homestead there is exactly one trader who is interested in it at the given price. We have found a competitive equilibrium

Underlying the definition of competitive equilibrium, we have a story about the way prices change: in a situation in which more than one trader would like a certain homestead, its price rises; and when no trader wants it, the price goes down. One can imagine an announcer declaring the prices, revising them, and revising again and again… until, wonder of wonders, each homestead has a single trader who is still interested in it and can afford it. But there are only a few markets that have such an announcer. In the absence of an announcer, the long arm of the **invisible hand** operates, steering the prices toward competitive equilibrium.

Does a competitive equilibrium always exist? The following claim states that whatever the traders' preferences and the initial state of ownership, there is always at least one equilibrium.

Market Claim 1: A competitive equilibrium always exists.

> **Proof:** We will prove the claim by constructing an algorithm that always leads to a competitive equilibrium.

We will call a "cycle" any sequence of traders in which each trader prefers most the homestead of the trader who follows him in the series, with the last trader preferring the homestead of the first trader. How do we know that such a cycle exists? We will arbitrarily choose one of the traders,(let us call him Trader 1). The homestead he prefers most is the homestead belonging to a trader called Trader 2. Trader 2 prefers most the homestead of Trader 3 and Trader 3 prefers most the homestead of Trader 4. We will continue on until we again reach a trader who has already appeared in the chain. For example, if Trader 4 prefers the homestead of Trader 2, then we identify the cycle: Trader 2 → Trader 3 → Trader 4 → Trader 2. If Trader 4 prefers his own homestead, we get a so-called degenerate cycle: Trader 4 → Trader 4. We will assign a single arbitrary price to each of the homesteads owned by the traders in the cycle.

We will continue the algorithm without the homesteads whose prices we just set and without their initial owners. At every stage, we will identify a cycle of traders in which each trader regards the homestead held by the next trader in the cycle as the best of the homesteads that were not allocated during the earlier stages. We will assign to the homesteads of the traders in the cycle a lower price than the prices assigned to the homesteads in the earlier stages. We will allocate the homesteads whose prices we just set and their initial owners and we will continue this as long as traders and homesteads remain.

The algorithm can progress in various ways, but eventually it has to end because at each stage at least one trader leaves the cycle (when he is allocated a homestead). In this way, we will create a series of cycles of trade and will assign prices to each of the homesteads. We assigned an identical price to each of the homesteads whose owners are in the same cycle. We assigned a lower price to a cycle we found at a later stage.

We will prove that this set of prices is one of competitive equilibrium. Given a set of prices, we will see that each homestead has a single trader who would like it.

A trader whose initial homestead is assigned price P considers purchasing a homestead from among the group of homesteads whose prices are not higher than P – that is, all of the homesteads whose owners were not involved in the previous cycles of trade. The algorithm built the series of cycles such that his preferred homestead, among those left in his cycle, is the one that belonged to the next trader in the cycle of trade at the start of trading. Thus, each homestead has a single trader who would like it: the trader who appears before its owner in the current cycle of trade.

We will illustrate the algorithm with the example of the six homesteads: A is most interested in the homestead of D, who is most interested in that of A. Therefore, A→ D→ A is a cycle of trade: each of the traders in the cycle is most interested in the homestead of the trader who comes after him. We will arbitrarily determine that the price of each of the two homesteads they own, Vineyard and Beach, is 25. After removing these two homesteads and their owners, we are left with four traders (B, C, E, F) and four homesteads (Oil, Tomb, Nightclub and Forest).

Trader	B	C	E	F
Ownership	Oil	Grave	Nightclub	Forest
Ranking				
1	Oil	Oil	Oil	Nightclub
2	Forest	Forest	Tomb	Oil
3	Nightclub	Nightclub	Forest	Tomb
4	Tomb	Tomb	Nightclub	Forest

We will continue in the same way. Among the homesteads that remain, Trader B is most interested in Oil, the homestead he already possesses. Therefore, B → B is a cycle. We will assign Oil a price of 21. Finally, we will identify the cycle of trade C → F→E → C. Of the remaining homesteads, C prefers the homestead of F, who follows him in the cycle; F prefers the homestead of E, who prefers that owned by C. We will set the price of Forest, Nightclub and Tomb (the homesteads owned by these traders) at 10 (or any number less than 21)… and we have finished.

The wealth of a trader in the market means his ability to choose a homestead from among many. The source of the wealth in the market is based on a meeting of interests among the traders. For example, A is very interested in D's homestead and D is very interested in A's. Their homesteads have a relatively high price. On the other hand, the fact that there is someone (F) who wants E's homestead very much does not guarantee that E will be wealthy; the market price of E's homestead may be low because there is no one who really wants F's homestead.

There are many price systems that have competitive equilibrium. Nonetheless, the following claim shows that the market model still has a single ending.

Market Claim 2: All competitive equilibria result in the same allocation (the proof of this claim is more complex than the other proofs in this chapter and the reader who is interested can find it in my article with Michele Piccione, "Equilibrium in the Jungle").

How impressive! The competitive equilibrium provides a single prediction of the final allocation of homesteads, an allocation that depends, of course, on the initial ownership of the homesteads and the traders' preferences.

The efficiency of the jungle equilibrium

The jungle equilibrium makes the use of force unnecessary. In equilibrium, no hero can or wants to take over a homestead held by another hero.

In our jungle, a hero's takeover of another hero's homestead by force is a legitimate action, but – unlike in the market – there are no mechanisms that allow a group of individuals to trade homesteads of their own volition. It is easy to imagine the unrest in the jungle if a number of heroes were to discover that they could enhance their situation if they adopted foreign ways and agreed among themselves on a round of homestead swaps. If they did this, the masses would accuse the economic system of the jungle of inefficiency and would demand reforms. The next claim shows that there is no reason for concern. Before formulating it, we will present one definition: an allocation is **efficient** if there is no cycle of homestead swaps between some of the heroes that would enhance the situation of all of those participating in the swap.

Jungle Claim 3: The jungle equilibrium is an efficient allocation.

> **Proof**: We start with a situation in which each hero possesses the homestead allocated to him in the jungle equilibrium.
>
> Let's look at any cycle of homestead swaps and focus on the strongest hero in the cycle. The homestead the hero holds after the swap is different from the one he held before the swap. Therefore, in equilibrium, the homestead must have been held by one of the

heroes weaker than him, as our hero is the strongest one participating. This homestead is necessarily less preferable for him than the homestead he possessed when in equilibrium: otherwise, he would have taken it over and the initial allocation would not have been an equilibrium.

Let's summarize: After the jungle reaches equilibrium, any cycle of homestead swaps would worsen the situation of at least one of the participating heroes. Therefore, the allocation of the jungle equilibrium is efficient.

Until now, we assumed that each hero is concerned only with the homestead he owns and does not care which ones the other heroes own. In reality, the situation is sometimes different and the location of each hero affects the welfare of another hero. For example, we all want the strongest ones to live in the outlying areas so they can protect us from our enemies. A matter of concern for many of us is who lives in the neighboring homestead. In the language of economists, we say this is a situation where externalities exist. In such circumstances, the jungle equilibrium may not have the attribute of efficiency.

We will illustrate this point with an example:

Consider a jungle that has three heroes: A, B and C, and three homesteads: Beach, Forest and Oil. There are six possible allocations of homesteads to heroes. Let's say that Hero A is stronger than Hero B, and Hero B is stronger than Hero C. The table below shows how the three heroes rank the six possible allocations. Each allocation is denoted by a threesome. For example, the threesome (Forest, Oil, Beach) denotes the allocation in which A settles in Forest, B in Oil and C in Beach.

Hero	A	B	C
1	(Forest, Oil, Beach)**	(Oil, Forest, Beach)	(Forest, Oil, Beach)**
2	(Beach, Oil, Forest)	(Oil, Beach, Forest)	(Oil, Forest, Beach)
3	(Beach, Forest, Oil)*	(Forest, Beach, Oil)	(Beach, Oil, Forest)
4	(Oil, Forest, Beach)	(Forest, Oil, Beach)**	(Oil, Beach, Forest)
5	(Forest, Beach, Oil)	(Beach, Forest, Oil)*	(Beach, Forest, Oil)*
6	(Oil, Beach, Forest)	(Beach, Oil, Forest)	(Forest, Beach, Oil)

Note that Hero C is primarily concerned with the homestead he receives. On the other hand, Heroes A and B also attribute importance to the homestead in which the other heroes settle. Each of them wants the other to settle in the Oil homestead.

The definition of equilibrium in the jungle with externalities is a bit subtle. The hero who sets out to grab a different homestead must take into consideration not only which homestead to choose; he must consider also how the displaced hero will react. Here, we'll assume that the evicted hero moves to the homestead of the hero who evicted him. Thus, we'll say that the allocation is a jungle equilibrium if there is no hero who prefers the allocation that would result from an exchange of homesteads with a weaker hero. For example, the allocation marked in the table with two asterisks (**) is not a jungle equilibrium. B could impose a swap with C and the result of this exchange (Forest, Beach, Oil) is ranked higher by B than the allocation marked by two asterisks.

The allocation marked with one asterisk (*) is an equilibrium allocation, but it is not an efficient allocation: the three heroes prefer the allocation with the two asterisks. It is possible to implement a more efficient allocation, but in order to do this the government would need to declare the Beach homestead a closed military area and use its power to ensure the allocation of Beach to C.

Yes, we are proud that the anarchy of the jungle usually leads to an efficient allocation, but we recognize that there are circumstances in which government intervention is necessary.

The efficiency of competitive equilibrium

Competitive equilibrium is defined by the existence of a price list in which each homestead has a single trader who is interested in acquiring it and able to do so. We will now see that the action of the invisible hand which leads to a competitive equilibrium also achieves the virtue of **Pareto efficiency**: there is no other allocation of homesteads to traders that would benefit some of them without being detrimental to any others. (Incidentally, under the conditions of the model, this characteristic is equivalent to what we called efficiency in the jungle.) Achieving Pareto efficiency is a central goal of our economy. An allocation that is not Pareto efficient is not a good allocation because it is possible to improve the welfare of at least some of the individuals without this coming at the expense of one of the other individuals. The following statement (which is called in the economic literature the first fundamental theorem of welfare economics) stipulates that the market mechanism achieves the ideal of efficiency.

Market Claim 3: The allocation in a competitive equilibrium is Pareto efficient.

> **Proof**: We'll start with a competitive equilibrium allocation. Let's consider some other allocation. We'll

call a trader differentiated if he receives two different homesteads in the two allocations. We will focus on differentiated Trader X, who possesses the most expensive of the homesteads held by the differentiated traders in equilibrium. In the new allocation, he received a homestead held in equilibrium by another differentiated trader, Y, and the price of the homestead Y held in equilibrium is not higher than the price of the homestead X held in equilibrium (because X is the richest of the differentiated traders). Consequently, given equilibrium prices, X could have acquired the homestead assigned to him in the new allocation but nonetheless refrained from doing so. This means that he values this homestead less than the homestead he held in equilibrium.

Let's summarize: After the market reaches competitive equilibrium, any other allocation, even if it is advantageous to some of the traders, is detrimental to at least one of the others. Therefore, the allocation of competitive equilibrium is Pareto efficient.

There is usually no need for the government to intervene and disrupt the market forces from doing their work. But we realize that there are exceptional situations in which Pareto efficiency is not achieved and there are grounds for considering government intervention in the market mechanism, for instance by offering benefits to traders to settle in sensitive regions. These situations might arise, for example, when there are traders who care not only about their own location, but also about the location of the other traders. In the language of economists, we say that this is a situation in which externalities are present. In such a case, there is room for payment to traders who settle in sensitive regions. We will elaborate in another course.

We noted that sometimes competitive equilibrium does not lead to efficiency, but we forgot to teach this fact to the devoted supporters of the market economy, who continue to cite the first fundamental theorem of welfare economics without mentioning that its conclusion is based on the assumption that an individual's welfare depends solely on the homestead he obtains.

Summary of the first lecture on the jungle economy

I hope that the first lecture was not too intensive, despite the fact that I crammed a summary of the entire course into it. Before I conclude the lecture, allow me to make a few more comments.

Yes, we are proud of the fact that our economic system compensates the strongest heroes, and that the weaker ones receive only the stronger ones' leftovers. Our economic system encourages people not to be weaklings. The School of Economics is named after mighty Samson. Our business school awards the MBA degree to those who have specialized in taking over the assets of others in elegant and original ways. Our best people devote their energies to the army, security, and the construction of walls and fences, and do not waste their talents on *luftgeschäft*, pie in the sky ideas.

It is true that in order for the jungle economy to function, the heroes need to clearly identify who is stronger than whom. In the jungle, Valentine's Day is the Festival of Strength and not of love. On that day, all of the heroes gather and wrestle until they collapse from exhaustion, or... until night falls. At night, fatigued but standing proud, the heroes line up in a row in the moonlight, ranked from strongest to weakest. At first glance, it seems like a meaningless ancient pagan ritual. But we, the economists, have discovered the logic behind this tradition: its objective is to let all the heroes know who is strong and who is weak in the jungle. In this way, our economy can function without unnecessary friction. You see, economics has just as much to say about anthropological issues as it has to contribute to so-called economic issues.

True, the use of power to grease the wheels of our economy sometimes leaves victims in its wake. Our heroes are also human and sometimes make mistakes. A weak hero sometimes gets confused, fails to recognize his weakness, and resists when a stronger hero demands that he evacuate his homestead. A commotion ensues and the stronger hero must resort to force – reasonable force, of course – to remind the weaker hero of his inferior standing. In the language of economists, we call the damages incurred in such clashes transaction costs. We will remember the victims of the jungle economy, upon whose backs the system was built, and continue on.

Of course, we understand the feelings of the social lobby which is frustrated that the jungle economy is liable to generate an unfair allocation. Those who have asthma or who suffer from humidity in the summer prefer to live far from the sea. If the asthmatic is weaker, the outcome of the jungle economy will be unjust. Alas, the jungle is green, but it is not the Garden of Eden.

To summarize the first lecture in the Introduction to Jungle Economics course: we showed that the laws of the jungle lead to a stable and efficient outcome, without markets, without money, without commercial law and almost without the need for government intervention.

Summary of the first lecture in the market economy

I know that the first lecture of the course was quite a load. No wonder. My colleagues say, with a wink, that the Introduction to Market Economics course contains all the ideas an economist really needs to understand. Before I conclude the lecture, I would like to add a few more points.

Some argue against us that our system encourages people to be greedy and hedonistic. That is not true. We have a marginal influence on the nature of human beings. Human beings bring credit to evolution. By nature, they always aspire to obtain the best of what is possible. Many people engage in a feverish search for business opportunities. When someone is ready to sell something at a low price and someone else is willing to buy it at a high price, there will always be someone who immediately identifies the opportunity to buy from the former and sell to the latter.

A system of prices can be created without the need for a centralized mechanism to manage commerce. You will ask: how does the market arrive at equilibrium prices? This mystery is the magic behind our economic system.

The commerce in the market entails transaction costs – the time and effort needed to identify and execute a transaction. But these are negligible costs that we can ignore, and we can move on.

We will sadly note the sense of frustration among members of the social lobby, who argue that the laws of the marketplace ignore considerations of fairness. If someone who suffers from asthma and someone who is allergic to sweat in the summer would benefit by living in a homestead far from the sea, but the desirable homestead is owned by a wimp who happened to inherit it from his parents, then the outcome of the market is unjust. Yes, alas, the market is only *almost* the Garden of Eden.

To summarize the first lecture on the market economy, we will say only: behold, look and see how great are the wonders of the market.

End

The presentation of the two Introduction to Economics lectures is over. In one lecture, the model of the market took center stage. It is a familiar model that is taught in every Department of Economics. It is conventionally regarded as a basis for understanding the economic world in which we live, even though it is quite unrealistic, imaginary, does not provide an explanation for the wonder of equilibrium prices, and its predictive qualities are limited. The other lecture focused on the model of the jungle, a model that does not appear in the textbooks and seems to be taken from a Walt Disney movie, completely detached from the developed world in which we live.

Is the jungle economy relevant only to cultures that are far from us in place and time? I'm afraid not. Here is a scenario that does not sound imaginary to me at all: as a result of climate change and the proliferation of nuclear weapons, the great Gog and Magog apocalypse erupts. The survivors do not need any consumer product except for a magic capsule called manna that falls from heaven every morning. Some people are unfortunate and nothing good ever falls upon them from above. Others are lucky, groaning under mountains of manna. In this post-traumatic world, those who lack manna try to use physical force to take what they need to subsist from those who have an abundance of manna. The market mechanism cannot be used for an exchange of goods because in this world there are no goods other than manna. At most, the market mechanism can regulate the barter of manna and strength; the owners of manna pay some of those who lack manna to physically protect them. A version of the jungle model would describe this world better than the model of the market.

But even without such a horrible scenario, the jungle model is more relevant to our world than might appear at first glance. Physical strength constitutes an influential factor also in the contemporary economy. Property crimes are aggressive actions in which assets are transferred from individuals to individuals. The bully in the prison cell gets the best bed and this is also true in many decent families. Strength played an important role in the allocation of assets in regimes that have collapsed. Nations have robbed and continue to rob other nations by exercising military power.

But when we speak about the use of force as a factor that determines the distribution of goods in a society, we are referring not only to military power. In our world, it is not uncommon for people to use gentle force to allocate goods, and in some cases we do not even see anything wrong with this. The power of rank determines the parking arrangements even at universities. The power of seniority determines priority in awarding special privileges in elite army units and in nursing homes. The power of persuasion leads participants in negotiations to agree to what they are not interested in. And let's not forget the power of attraction, male or female, that drives the process of allocating men to women and vice versa. Let's say He-1 is with She-1 and He-2 is with She-2. But now He-1 prefers She-2 to his present partner, bless her soul, and He-1 is more attractive than He-2. So He-1 appears before She-2, exercises his manly powers – and the deal is closed. I shudder at the thought of using the market mechanism to make matches between the sexes.

The models presented in the two Introduction to Economics lectures are nothing but fables. Neither of them describes reality, but both of them still describe something from reality. Neither of them provides an unequivocal argument in favor or against this or that economic system, but studying both of them together helps to some extent in understanding economic mechanisms.

I have attempted to present the two models, side by side, as symmetrically as possible. My main objective was to promote a critique of the way in which we teach economics in universities. The study of economics conventionally focuses on the market model which quickly captivates the hearts of the students, not as a result of empirical evidence or following proper discussion — these are usually absent. Students of economics are enchanted by the elegance of the market model, by its decisiveness, and by its ability to predict, whether correctly or erroneously. In this chapter, I have tried to emphasize how easy it is to impress students, by using similar tools and employing rhetorical ploys with a different economic system, a system that is not to my liking either.

4. Economics, Pragmatics and Seven Traps

A visit to interdisciplinary realms

The writing of this book is replete with doubts for me. I am discussing academic issues from a personal perspective, a very personal one. While attracted to this form of writing, I do not feel completely at ease with it. In all of my academic work, I have wrapped myself in formal models of economic theory, game theory and decision theory. Typical titles of my papers were: "A Bargaining Model with Incomplete Information" and "Comments on the Interpretation of Decision Problems with Imperfect Recall." So how is it that I have stooped to using the expression "a visit to interdisciplinary realms"? If I am not careful, the interdisciplinary realms will spill into the realms of my childhood, with its intercultural nature explaining my interest in interdisciplinary subjects. And with a little imagination, I am liable even to revisit my mythological grocer (behold – he is already here again).

The pretense of the current visit to interdisciplinary realms is to illustrate how economic thinking can contribute to the analysis of issues that are not economic. I will embark on this visit with a critical outlook that will help me to recognize traps and perhaps even search for them. Some of the traps are unique to interdisciplinary research, while others can also be found in other contexts. I will occasionally stray from the main objective of the discussion and draw the reader's attention to a trap, one, two, three… up to seven.

Economics is surrounded by interdisciplinary realms. The combinations of economics with sociology, zoology, criminology, psychology, law, political science, history and brain science, adorn the names of academic journals and advanced courses. I know economists who work on such combinations and wholeheartedly believe that economics has a lot to learn from other academic fields. But, in general, it seems to me that the spread of economics to other areas derives from the view expressed by the economist Steven Levitt: "Economics is a science with excellent tools for gaining answers, but a serious shortage of interesting questions."

In conversations in departmental lounges or at post-seminar dinners, economists admit that economics is an imperialist profession. The giggling of those present when someone uses the expression "the imperialism of economics" is replaced by growing embarrassment when others begin to speak with arrogance and disdain about the natives in the colonies – that is, toward anyone who has yet to discover the treasures of economic thinking.

I am not a "patriot" of economics and I harbor no professional colonialist ambitions whatsoever. But I too have tried to work in interdisciplinary realms, first in economics and law and later in economics and language. I was drawn to such areas because they offer the prospect of ground-breaking innovation, originality and diversity. On days when I felt reservations about engaging in economics proper, I found an abandoned territory in the interdisciplinary realms – a refuge for economics without economics.

Consider **economics and law**. The field includes areas such as corporate law, antitrust law and tax law which reflect research in economics into the structure of the firm, industrial organization and public economics. But a different meaning of economics and law is of greater interest to me, and is related to my view that economic theory aims to clarify the logic of interactions between the individuals in a society. There is no reason for economic theory to restrict itself to economic interactions only. The legal system is also designed to organize the interactions between individuals in a society. And indeed, the field of economics and law examines the legal system with the tools we use to analyze economic systems. In this sense, the field employs the method of economic thinking, not the economic content.

Economics and language sounds a stranger combination. Language theory does not address economic problems. Here, economists assume the right to deal with topics that are supposed to be the purview of linguists and philosophers of language, based on the view that economics focuses on understanding how all social institutions function. When we use the term **social institution**, we are referring to the prevailing mechanisms and conventions in society that organize the interaction between individuals. What is a more fundamental social mechanism for cooperation between human beings than language? This gives rise to the urge to explain language in the same way as classical economic theory explains familiar economic mechanisms.

Even after the previous two paragraphs, I doubt whether the reader has gained even the slightest idea of how economic thinking is relevant to other fields. Instead of continuing with abstract explanations, it would be more effective to present one interdisciplinary economic study from the field of economics and language. The study to be presented here is a project I conducted jointly with my colleague Jacob (Kobi) Glazer. The project deals with situations of argument and persuasion. I was attracted to this project because it brought to mind childhood dreams that I have not fulfilled: to become an attorney for the oppressed and to win public debates on fateful issues. One advantage in discussing this particular project is that I was involved in it, and thus I am entitled to be critical without worrying about being accused of persecuting someone on a personal basis.

I have yet to say a word about economics and language and I am already talking about what attracted me to the field. It is not obvious why one would be attracted to interdisciplinary research. This seduces us to probe into the reasons that lead a person to this particular endeavor. So here, I have already stepped onto one landmine.

Trap 1: Research in interdisciplinary realms elicits personal exposure whose place in academic writing is doubtful.

Conversation and persuasion situations

We are entering an area that lies between economics and pragmatics. We have spoken about economics. Pragmatics is a branch of linguistics that deals with the rules guiding the implications of things said in a conversation (utterances). Pragmatics seeks to decipher the mechanisms that operate in our minds when we listen to a conversation like this one:

First conversation:

A: (who is in Jerusalem, is about to travel to London and is speaking on the telephone with B, who is in London): I can't wait to stroll around in the streets of London. Tell me, is the weather stormy there?

B: It's not raining hard.

B's statement – if detached from the context in which it was spoken – does not rule out the possibility that it is not raining at all in London. Nonetheless, in the context of the conversation, the clear meaning of B's statement is that it is raining in London, but not hard. What are the principles that lead us to understand this statement so unambiguously?

Second conversation:

C: (outside the conference room, speaking by phone to D, who is inside the conference room): Who is participating in the meeting?

D: Most of the people I see are economists.

D did not mention participants who are not economists. In fact, he did not say that he was looking at participants in the conference room at all (and not, for example, at passersby seen from the window of the room).

Nonetheless, we have no doubt that D meant to say that most of the participants at the meeting are economists, while some of the participants are not economists. How is it so clear to us that this is what D intended to say?

Pragmatics clarifies the rules that are engraved in our minds, which make these deductions so self-evident, without our even being aware that these rules exist. The high priest of pragmatics is the philosopher Paul Grice, whose main thesis is the **cooperative principle**: the rules that we employ to understand statements spoken during an everyday conversation derive from the assumption that the speaker and the listener have shared interests, and the conversation they conduct is intended to promote these interests. Grice deduces from the cooperative principle that the meaning of a statement in a conversation must be consistent with the assumption that the speaker intends to convey to the listener information that is correct, relevant, and sufficiently detailed, in the simplest possible way.

Grice's approach reminds us of the approach used in economics to explain and understand social institutions. We imagine a super planner who has designed a social institution in order to promote a reasonable objective. We aspire to show that a familiar social institution optimally fulfills the objective of this social designer. Well, this aspiration may be a bit exaggerated. We will be satisfied if we show that the familiar social institution shares important characteristics with the social institution the social designer would have selected.

Let's return to the first conversation. B takes the trouble to say "It's not raining hard," and does not suffice with the shorter statement, "It's not raining." This indicates that he wanted to convey something more. What could he have meant? That it is raining and it is not pouring. And why didn't he say "It's raining, but not hard?" Because B wanted to be relevant and knew that what was troubling A was that if it poured he would not be able to enjoy a stroll through the city. The two utterances "It's not raining hard" and "It's raining, but not hard" are not identical. But in the context of the conversation, the rules of pragmatics make them carry the same meaning.

In the second conversation, because D is supposed to be relevant, we deduce that D is responding to C's question and is referring to the group of people that C is interested in – that is, the group of participants in the meeting. Thus, D intends to say that most of the people in the conference room are economists. He could have stated more informatively (and just as simply): "All of the participants in the meeting are economists." The fact that he did not say this leads us to deduce that that statement would not have been correct and that most – but not all – of the participants in the meeting are economists.

Grice's rules refer to conversation situations. In this chapter, we are interested in what we call a **persuasion situation**. A persuasion situation, like a conversation, involves an exchange of words. What characterizes a persuasion situation is that someone (we'll call him **the petitioner**) seeks to persuade someone else (we'll call him **the listener**) to adopt his opinion or perform an action. Examples of persuasion situations include: a worker tries to convince an employer to hire him, a politician seeks the public's trust, or a telephone company attempts to convince a customer to switch over from the rival company. We are interested in identifying the principles that determine what constitutes a convincing argument in a persuasion situation and how utterances aimed at persuading someone are interpreted. In other words, we are interested in developing a theory of pragmatics that applies to persuasion situations.

Examining intuition

Our starting point (Kobi's and mine) was routine observation of the world. Everyday, we participate in or witness persuasion situations in the family, in the workplace, in the market and in politics. We noticed that the meaning we attribute to a statement made in a persuasion situation is often different than the meaning we would assign to the same statement if made in an ordinary, non-persuasive, conversation. When the listener interprets a statement in a persuasion situation, he is aware of the fact that the persuader is trying hard to convince him. He thinks strategically (in the sense discussed in the chapter on game theory) and takes into consideration not only what the petitioner says, but also what the petitioner chooses to say and what not to say.

But, unlike philosophers and linguists, we economists behave as if we do not rely solely on our impressions of the world and introspection. We aspire to reinforce our impressions via experiments that usually — surprise surprise! — support our intuitions, at least in the cases that are reported. Will this also be true here?

We asked students and lecturers in several universities around the world to relate to two stories. It cannot be said that these stories are taken from actual events though they bring to mind realistic situations. In experiments, as in models, the world is refined to the point of absurdity. We refrain from confronting the respondents with situations that are too familiar or complex. Familiar situations are not suitable because the respondents are liable to be influenced by factors specific to their own lives, but irrelevant to our study. A complex situation is liable to be incomprehensible, especially to respondents who did us a favor by participating in the experiment and have a limited attention span (you can experiment with these situations on the book's website: http://www.openbookpublishers.com/exsites/136).

> **First story**: Imagine that you are one of two players in the following game. There are two packs of cards in the game. Each pack contains 100 cards, numbered from 1 to 100. Two cards, one from each pack, are selected randomly and given to the other player. Only he sees the numbers on the two cards. His aim is to persuade you that the sum of the two cards in his hand is higher than 100. He can show you only one of the two cards. You have to guess whether or not the sum of the cards is higher than 100. The other player will receive a prize if he succeeds in persuading you that the sum of the numbers on the two cards is greater than 100. You will receive a prize if your guess turns out to be correct.
>
> The other player showed you a card with the number 59. What is your guess: Is the sum of the cards in the other player's hand higher than 100, or not?

In this story, you are the listener and the other player is the petitioner. The story brings to mind realistic situations such as the following: a candidate for employment (the petitioner) tries to persuade an employer (the listener) to hire him. The candidate has two references from previous employers. The content of the letters can range from an enthusiastic recommendation (like the 100 card) to a scathing critique (like the 0 card). The employer does not have the time to read both of them and asks the candidate to give him just one of them (like the constraint in the story where the player can only show one card). The applicant claims that the references from his two former employers place him above the average candidate (comparable to the player claiming that the sum of the cards he holds is greater than 100). He presents a reference that is slightly better than the average (comparable to the card with the number 59). And finally, the question of whether or not the presentation of this reference supports the candidate's chance of getting the job is comparable to the question of how to interpret the fact that the player chose to show the 59 card.

I can think of two conflicting considerations the listener might have in mind after the 59 card is presented as evidence designed to persuade him that the sum of the two cards is greater than 100.

> **Naïve consideration**: The listener sees the display of the 59 card as an innocent move and does not take into consideration the fact that the petitioner chose to display this card and not the other one. For the sum of the cards to be greater than 100, the number on the second card must be at least 42. The listener is aware that the second card was drawn from a pack containing 100 cards, numbered 1 to 100. He calculates the probability that the number on the second card is 42 or higher (59%) and the probability that the second

card is lower than 42 (41%), and concludes that it is more probable that the sum of the numbers on the two cards is greater than 100.

Strategic consideration: The listener asks himself what led the petitioner to display the 59 card. He is aware of the fact that the petitioner is trying to persuade him that the sum of the numbers is higher than 100 and therefore did not show him just any card, but instead chose to show the card with the higher number of the two in his hand. Consequently, the listener deduces that the second card has a number less than 59. If so, the chance of the second card having a number between 42 and 59 (which would bring the sum above 100), i.e., 18/59, is smaller than the chance of the second card having a number between 1 and 41 (too small to make the sum of the two cards greater than 100), i.e., 41/59. Therefore, it is more probable that the sum of the numbers on the cards in his hand does not exceed 100.

So, do people interpret the display of the 59 card as evidence that supports the petitioner or as evidence against his argument? Our sample included more than 1,500 respondents. Some 43% of them apparently exercised the naïve consideration and deduced that the sum of the cards was greater than 100. Most of the respondents, 57%, exercised the strategic consideration and deduced that the sum of the two cards did not exceed 100.

What would happen if the statement "one of the cards is the 59 card" is uttered during a conversation between two people and not in a persuasion situation? Imagine, for example, that two people are talking on the phone. One of them holds the two cards in his hand. The two people have a shared interest in determining whether the sum of the cards is greater than 100. The person holding the cards says to the other one: "The number on one card is 59 and the number on…" and at that moment, before the speaker has a chance to mention the number on the second card, the conversation is cut off. The listener is left to guess whether or not the sum of the cards is higher than 100. Unlike in the persuasion situation, the great majority of those asked to interpret the statement ("The number on one card is 59") guess that the sum of the cards is greater than 100. It seems that in a conversation, the listener believes that the speaker decided randomly which of the two cards to take first and not necessarily the higher card.

> **Second story**: You are speaking with someone about the change in the level of education in major cities in the world. You are very eager to persuade him that the level of education has risen during the past decade in most cities in the world. You tell him that you have reports about the trends in the level of education in Brussels, Cairo, Manila and Mexico City. He says that he saw a reliable report indicating that the level of education in Bangkok declined during the past decade. All of your four reports support your contention, but you only have time to show him information on just one of these four cities. Presenting information on which of the four would strengthen your position most?

The story describes a persuasion situation. You are the petitioner. Now that Bangkok has been presented as a counter-argument to your contention, you are expected to respond with an argument that is "proximate" to the argument made about Bangkok. In this context, most people think about proximity in the geographic sense and the listener expects to hear from you about the level of education in a city near Bangkok – in our case that would be Manila. So if you present the report on Mexico City, the listener will deduce that the report on Manila does not support your contention. He will know that one case (Mexico City), supports your position, while two other cases (Bangkok and Manila) do not. If you present the details of the report on Manila, the listener will not draw any conclusion about the level of education in any of the other cities. He will then have data that supports your position in one case (Manila) and does not support your position in another case (Bangkok). Therefore, your situation will be better if you present the report on Manila.

The findings support our intuition: in a survey conducted among about 600 students, 51% of the respondents said that Manila was the most persuasive argument, compared to 23% who selected Mexico City and 13% who chose Cairo and Brussels. And this is despite the fact that Manila is not the most prominent of the four cities. When we replaced Bangkok with Amsterdam, 71% of the respondents selected Brussels as the best argument, with the rest of the votes split evenly between the three other cities.

A different interpretation would be attributed to this conversation if it were simply conducted between two inquisitive people rather than in the context of a persuasion situation. Let's say that at the beginning of the discussion it becomes apparent that the level of education in Bangkok had declined (and incidentally we conducted the experiment before I visited Bangkok, when I learned that the level of education had actually risen there in the last few years). Let's assume that one of the interlocutors is knowledgeable about the level of education in the four cities (Brussels, Cairo, Manila and Mexico City) and he mentions that the level of education in Mexico City has risen. I doubt that this statement would be taken in any way other than literally. No one would deduce anything about the level of education in the other cities based on the fact that the speaker chose to cite Mexico City as an example.

It seems that most of the respondents, in regard to both stories, took into consideration the fact that the petitioner chose what to say and what not to say, and that his choice was made with the goal of persuading the listener.

In the first story, the petitioner presents evidence – the card with the number 59. Ostensibly all he said was "I have a card with the number 59," but most of the respondents say to themselves that the speaker is rational and was doing his best to persuade the listener. If the speaker held a more convincing card, he would have shown it. Consequently, the respondents deduce that the speaker was unable to show a card with a higher number and, therefore, the sentence "I have a card with the number 59" means that "The highest number appearing on the cards in my hand is 59."

In the second story, after the listener tells the petitioner that the case of Bangkok does not support his position, the petitioner is expected to refer to Manila, the only city on the list that can be said to be geographically close to Bangkok. The most convincing argument is: "the level of education in Manila has risen." That is, if the petitioner had argued for example, "the level of education in Brussels has risen", this statement would have been interpreted as if he had presented a weaker argument, "the level of education has risen in Brussels, but not in Manila."

Criticism (1)

Of course, I am happy about the faith that you, the readers, have shown in me by unquestioningly accepting the survey results I reported. But what do you know about the method by which the survey was conducted? Who were the respondents and to what extent do the responses of several hundred students reflect the general population? Do I also report experiments that did not succeed or only those whose results support what I want to show? Don't you have a sneaking feeling that I have an interest in bending the results a bit in order to appear – to myself as well as to you – as more persuasive?

In fact, you the readers and I are involved in a persuasion situation right now. I want to convince you that the results of the survey support the thesis that I am presenting here. I must not lie, but I can choose to highlight only the findings that support my thesis and to hide the less favorable ones. This is the situation in all experimental and empirical work. The researcher wants to appear wise, correct and original – regardless of the quality of his research.

If we are interested in verified facts, we should look at findings with a measure of skepticism. But most of us prefer not to delve into the experimental and empirical data or examine how researchers reached their conclusions.

The culture of relying on someone is especially prevalent in the interdisciplinary realms. We are not sufficiently critical when we cite research conducted in another field, because we are not knowledgeable enough to do so; often the citation is just intended to demonstrate the breadth of our horizons. We are also insufficiently critical in regard to citations from our own field, perhaps because we are interested in impressing researchers from other fields, and fear that by criticizing the works of other economists we may harm ourselves too.

If economists would write models describing the research in economics and would include economists among the decision makers, they would certainly adopt the approach that the conclusions should not be taken at face value, and that the interests of the researchers should be taken into account. Economists would discuss the incentives they face when they collect, analyze and publish findings. They would also speak about the common interests of the members of the economics club to praise themselves in front of spectators from the other clubs. But the economists do not write models about economists. Only rarely have I heard an economist complain that a colleague who had announced a great discovery in his famous article, had been selective in his choice of the findings he presented, and had omitted data that was not quite consistent with his discovery. In other words, we have encountered another trap.

Trap 2: We are unduly impressed by studies published in the professional journals and pay too little attention to the personal interests of the researchers.

The economists are coming

What principles determine the difference between a convincing and a non-convincing statement? Let's return to my study with Kobi. The basic premise of our approach is that there is truth in the world. If the listener knew this truth, there would be no need for a persuasion process and the listener would adopt or reject the petitioner's position in accordance with the truth and according to his preferences. However, the truth is not known to the listener. Only the petitioner knows the relevant facts and, independent of the truth, he is always interested in convincing the listener of something. The listener, on the other hand, would like to be persuaded by the petitioner's arguments only under certain conditions. The situation becomes charged with tension similar to that present in many typical economic situations. The petitioner and the listener have common interests, as there are circumstances in which it is beneficial for the listener to accede to the petitioner. But there are also conflicts of interest, and there are circumstances in which it is best for the listener to reject the petitioner's arguments. This is why Grice's **cooperative principle** is not a reasonable basis for a theory explaining the rules used to interpret statements in a persuasion situation. We will therefore try to formulate an alternative principle that can explain the rules people use naturally when interpreting a petitioner's arguments in a persuasion situation.

In our approach, the purpose of the persuasion process is to enable the listener to extract from the petitioner as much of the information he needs as possible. We assume that a social designer implanted in human beings the rules with which they interpret the arguments and evidence presented in a persuasion situation. The designer assumed that the petitioner would act in a rational way and that the listener would listen to the petitioner and act according to the rules of persuasion implanted in him by the designer. The designer chose rules of persuasion that maximize the chance that the listener will reach the correct conclusion from his own perspective.

The social designer determines which arguments will convince the listener and which will not. He must take into consideration certain limitations: time limitations – the listener has very little spare time; and cognitive limitations – there is a limit to the listener's ability to absorb and digest data and draw conclusions. As we know, even the judicial system is cognizant of the severe time constraints in which the courts operate and the limits of judge's ability to absorb and process information, even in a life and death situation.

Who is this super-designer who defines our life for us and whose optimization will be the cornerstone to our analysis? In the best of the economic tradition, we are speaking of a "virtual" designer. If we insist on removing the mask from this mysterious figure, we will hide behind the term "evolutionary forces". In some contexts (for example, when the listener is the boss), we might say that the designer is the listener himself; thanks to his strong position vis-à-vis the petitioner, he is the one who decides on the rules of the game. But, perhaps it is best to admit:

Trap 3: Actually, we are not really sure what we are doing...

Our approach leads us to clothe the problem of the virtual designer in formal dress. We will then analyze the formal model, swept up in the magic of transforming a mysterious, vague issue into a clear mathematical problem. This is not the place for a detailed description of the formal model – that is the domain of the professional literature. Here, we will suffice with presenting a simple example, just a taste of the model.

Actually, even if I were to write about this subject in the professional interdisciplinary literature, I would suffice with a concise presentation of the essence of the model. I would not go into great detail on linguistic issues because I am not expert enough to delve into their complexities. I would also not go into too much detail in describing the formal model, because it would deter readers who are not well-versed in economic theory. So, in other words, my own words have led me into another trap.

> **Trap 4: In the interdisciplinary realms, the presentations must be concise. There is no room for details. We tend to speak about the general picture and often remain there.**

Building a model

A petitioner is interested in persuading a listener about a certain matter. He can make use of the opinions of five experts: A, B, C, D, and E. Each expert has an unequivocal opinion on the matter. He either supports the petitioner's position, or he opposes it. We will call the description of the opinions of the five experts – the **state of affairs**.

An example of a state of affairs: A, B and D support the petitioner's position, while C and E oppose it. There are $2 \times 2 \times 2 \times 2 \times 2 = 32$ possible states of affairs. If the listener were aware of the opinion of the five experts, he would be persuaded only if the majority of experts support the petitioner's position.

However, only the petitioner knows the opinion of the experts. In the persuasion process, the petitioner seeks to convince the listener that the state of affairs is such that it is worthwhile for him to accept the opinion of the petitioner. An important premise (and later we will discuss it at greater length) is that the petitioner is allowed to raise an argument that represents the opinion of two experts only. **A rule of persuasion** defines what is considered a convincing argument and what is perceived as a non-convincing argument. The petitioner, who is aware of the state of affairs and the rule of persuasion, will check whether there is an argument that he is allowed to voice and which will persuade the listener. If there is such an argument, the petitioner will raise it.

The petitioner is not permitted (in the model) to do anything except present the opinions of the experts. Thus, for example, he cannot curse, bang on the table or open fire… he cannot falsely claim that a certain expert supports his position when the expert does not support him. This is particularly relevant in a situation in which, beyond mere words about the experts' views, the petitioner must substantiate his statements with the reasoned declarations of the experts.

Finally, we come to that mysterious designer – the one responsible for choosing the rule of persuasion.

The rule of persuasion he chooses will apply in all states of affairs (since the listener, who uses the rule, does not distinguish between different states of affairs). In order to assess a rule of persuasion, the designer identifies the states of affairs in which the listener makes a decision that from the listener's perspective is the wrong one. The designer counts as a mistake (i) every state of affairs in which the listener does not want to be persuaded, yet the petitioner is able to persuade him to accept his position; and (ii) every state of affairs in which the listener would want to be persuaded, yet the rule of persuasion does not allow the petitioner to present a combination of convincing arguments. The designer does not distinguish between mistakes in the various states of affairs and attributes equal weight to each mistake. The central assumption of the model is that the designer chooses the rule of persuasion that minimizes the number of states of affairs in which the listener makes a decision that is wrong from his own perspective.

As stated, we allow the petitioner to present arguments that include the opinions of only two experts. The model would be uninteresting if we were to allow the petitioner to present the opinions of three experts. If that were the case, the social designer would determine that a convincing argument must cite three experts who support the petitioner. This rule of persuasion would always lead to the correct outcome from the listener's perspective. The premise of the model, stipulating that the petitioner can only refer to two experts, reflects the listener's limitations and prevents the social designer from imposing the full burden of proof on the petitioner.

The social designer in the model must choose one rule of persuasion from a large number of possibilities. Here are three examples of simple rules of persuasion:

1. The listener is convinced by the arguments of the petitioner if the petitioner can cite any two experts who support his position.

This rule of persuasion leads to an undesirable outcome from the perspective of the listener in 10 of the 32 states of affairs:

- In every state of affairs in which the listener would like to be persuaded – that is, when at least three of the five experts support the petitioner's position, the petitioner can convince the listener.
- The rule of persuasion prevents the petitioner from persuading the listener in the five states of affairs in which only a single expert supports the petitioner, as well as in the state of affairs in which all five experts oppose the petitioner's position. And indeed, the listener would not want to be persuaded in these six states of affairs.
- In the 10 states of affairs in which exactly two of the five experts support the petitioner, the petitioner can convince the listener to accept his position, despite the fact that the latter would prefer not to be persuaded.

2. Let's assume that the five experts are naturally arranged in the minds of the petitioner and the listener in the order A, B, C, D, E, as they appear, for example, in the directory of certified experts.

According to this rule of persuasion, the petitioner is not only required to cite two experts who support his position, but the two experts must also be "neighbors" (A and B, B and C, C and D, or D and E).

The rule of persuasion leads to a wrong result from the perspective of the listener in only five states of affairs:

- The petitioner can persuade the listener in all states of affairs in which three or more experts support his position, except for the one state of affairs in which only the experts A, C and E support him. (In this state of affairs, he cannot argue that some pair of neighboring experts supports his position.)

- The rule of persuasion prevents a mistake in the six states of affairs in which there is no pair of experts who support the petitioner.

- Of the 10 states of affairs in which only two experts support the petitioner, in four of them the experts are neighbors and the petitioner can convince the listener, despite the fact that he was not supposed to do this; in the other six states of affairs, the experts who support the petitioner are not neighbors and he has no way to convince the listener.

3. Let us assume that the five experts are arranged in the minds of the petitioner and the listener in two groups. A, B and C are in one group, and D and E in the second. This is the situation, for example, when the five experts are similar in every way,

except for the fact that three of them are men and two are women. The rule of persuasion requires the petitioner to provide evidence pertaining to two aspects of a same group (two men or two women). Citing the supporting opinions of B and C will convince the listener; on the other hand, citing the supporting opinions of A and D will not do so.

The third rule of persuasion limits the number of mistakes to 4:

- The petitioner can persuade the listener in all states of affairs in which at least three experts support him, because either two of the three are men or two of them are women.

- There are four problematic states of affairs in which the petitioner can convince the listener to accept his position, despite the fact that in these states of affairs the listener would prefer not to be persuaded: these four states of affairs are when exactly two experts support the petitioner's position and both of them are of the same sex (A and B, A and C, B and C, or D and E).

- In all of the other states of affairs, the number of experts supporting the petitioner is not greater than two; and if there are two experts who support the petitioner, they come from different groups. In these states of affairs, the petitioner has no way of persuading the listener and no mistake is generated.

What is the optimal rule of persuasion? It can be proven (we will not do this here) that every rule of persuasion involves at least four states of affairs in which the outcome of the persuasion situation will be wrong. Thus, third rule of persuasion, which is based on a division of the experts into two groups – one of three experts and the other of two experts – and which requires the petitioner to cite the views of two experts from the same group, is a rule of persuasion that minimizes the number of errors.

According to this optimal rule of persuasion, the argument citing the opinions of B and C in support of the petitioner convinces the listener, while the argument citing the opinions of B and D in support of the petitioner does not. The two arguments seemingly convey equal information (two of the five experts support the petitioner), but nonetheless are not equally convincing. When the social designer adopts the third rule of persuasion, the argument that cites B and D in support of the petitioner's position becomes more informative than it appears. The argument that B and D support the petitioner is interpreted as also admitting that there is no pair of supporting experts from the same group.

As noted, our approach is that the prevalent rules of persuasion in the real world derive from the maximization performed by the social designer. If there is any truth in our approach, we would expect to find the third rule of persuasion in persuasion situations in which there is a clear division of the experts into two groups, one of three and one of two. In the absence of such a single natural division, it will not be clear to the petitioner and the listener whether or not the two experts the petitioner cites come from the same group.

The model and reality

Is there really a connection between the optimal rule of persuasion and what people consider to be convincing? When a group of experts can be divided naturally into two groups of two and three experts, do people really find that citing testimony from two experts from the same group is more persuasive than citing testimony from two experts from different groups?

The third story does not deal with experts, but it is still easy to see the resemblance between the story and the model.

Third story: An exam consists of five questions printed on two separate pages, three on one page and two on the other. The questions were administered to many examinees and it was found that:

1. The fact that a person knows one answer does not indicate whether he knows another answer; and

2. About 50% of the examinees know the answer to every question.

You want to determine whether an examinee's ability is above the average in the population – that is, whether he is able to answer at least three questions. Due to time constraints, the examinee is asked to choose and answer only two questions.

Compare the following two events in terms of their ability to convince you that the examinee's knowledge is above average:

Event A: The examinee chose two questions, one from each page, and answered them correctly.

Event B: The examinee chose two questions from the page containing three questions and answered them correctly.

In the third story, each question reflects the examinee's level. In other words, each question functions like an expert in the model. The examinee is the petitioner and the examiner is the listener. The examinee's ability or inability to answer a question correctly is analogous to a situation in which an expert supports or opposes the petitioner's position. The examinee tries to persuade the examiner via the answers to only two questions that he knows the answers to at least three of the questions.

There is ostensibly no difference between the information received if the examinee answers two questions given on two different pages or if he answers two questions from a single page. Therefore, it would be possible to expect that the examiner would form the same opinion regardless of whether the examinee correctly answers two questions from two separate pages or two questions from the same page. However, according to our approach, an examinee who correctly answers two questions written on the same page should be considered more persuasive that an examinee who correctly answers two questions written on separate pages.

We presented the story to students and lecturers around the world. We asked them to compare the persuasiveness of Event A and Event B. We also allowed them to say that they find the two events equally persuasive. We expected to find that Event B would be perceived as more persuasive than Event A. Of 1,300 respondents, 28% found Event B to be more persuasive and 19% found Event A to be more persuasive.

Since the sample was a large one and 28% is much higher than 19%, it could be said that we received support for the conjecture that a correct answer on two questions from the same page is more convincing. But it can also surely be said that the results of the survey do not support our assumption because more than half of the respondents found the two events to be equal in terms of their persuasive power.

Criticism (2)

Our discussion focuses on a very specific case and therefore sheds little light on the rules of pragmatics in persuasion situations. Furthermore, the discussion lacks the depth and understanding necessary to try to formulate and explain the natural rules that guide us in understanding utterances in persuasion situations.

While recognizing the limitations of the model and the discussion, I found myself speaking about this study not only to economists and philosophers, but also to lawyers. Words such as: discussion, evidence, arguments and petition tempted me to hint about the possible implications of this approach for legal theory. I have nothing at the moment to contribute to legal thought, but this has not prevented me from reciting for years (and again, here and now) the mantra that it might be interesting to view legal procedure and the laws of evidence through the lenses of economic theory. While jumping from economics to linguistics, and from linguistics to the legal world, I recognized another trap.

Trap 5: The interdisciplinary worlds are like the universe. They have a tendency to expand nonstop.

And, incidentally, there is another troublesome aspect of this interdisciplinary expansion. Under pressure from the audience and market forces, universities are dragged into approving interdisciplinary programs of study at too early a stage in the student's academic career. In my view, an undergraduate student does not need to specialize. Instead, he should study a large number of areas from a list of basic fields such as: mathematics, philosophy, biology, history, physics, art, law and perhaps even economics. Challenging and provocative interdisciplinary studies should play a prominent role only in the course of studies for higher degrees, after the student has absorbed the forms of thinking from the basic fields.

Trap 6: The attractiveness of interdisciplinary studies leads students to engage in them at too early a stage in their studies, and thus prevents them from building a broad base of studies that can support a solid interdisciplinary pyramid.

Last trap

We have encountered six traps, jumped from economics to language and back, formulated bold assumptions (on a narrow base of knowledge) and played with a model. I will conclude the discussion with the last and most frightening trap of all.

Trap 7: Engaging in interdisciplinary realms without deep knowledge of the basic fields raises suspicion of charlatanism.

Now, it remains for me to wonder, perhaps in this chapter I fell into Trap 7 myself.

5. (Sort of) Economic Policy

Beginning

When I was a boy, I strolled every afternoon from my home through Shabbat Square toward the Workers' Library at the top of Strauss Street. Half-way up the hill was a kiosk that displayed all the daily newspapers, attached by clothes pegs to the wide-open metal window shutters. As a curious child, I would stop and read the newspapers, peeking under the corners of the pages until I had my fill, and then continuing on my way. My favorite two newspapers were always on the lower-left side. *Hamodia* – "the Mouthpiece of Ultra-Orthodox Jewry" – would vilify the police for brutally beating demonstrators at Shabbat Square. *Kol Ha'am* declared: "Workers of the world, unite!" and reported unpatriotically about border incidents. I became fond of both of them – perhaps because of their particularly bold typeface. Perhaps it was because both were slim, or perhaps because they gave voice to departed heroes my mother would mention with veneration: her brother, who would sit in the study hall of the Slonimer Hasidic Yeshiva until midnight; and her brother-in-law, who was a clandestine communist in Warsaw before the war.

We, who were born into the young State of Israel, grew up in the shadow of two cultures. One was Judaism, which we did not really know. But we were able to glean bits of it from our homes, from the street, from *bar mitzvah* preparations, and from what trickled into Israeli secular culture. The second was socialism, which we knew even less. We encountered its slogans on bulletin boards, in youth movement activity, and in what remained of the values of the Zionist socialist society after the establishment of the State of Israel. Both Judaism and socialism were regarded as absolute truths, great doctrines that provide answers to all questions, both intriguing and intimidating. We lived in a society that was trying to build a new type of "Israeliness," young and just, an antithesis of the past. But ultimately, I absorbed the message of solidarity not from the May Day parades, but on the eve of the Yom Kippur service.

At the Shalom Shachna Meisel synagogue, the children would jeer at me as someone who was not familiar with the prayer book. The librarian at the Workers' Union Library insulted me by chuckling when I asked to borrow Marx's *Das Capital*. I wandered between these two giant mountains, Judaism and Socialism, not climbing either one. I remained at the foot of these mountains, gazing up at them wonder.

Meanwhile, most of the newspapers hanging from the iron shutters of the kiosk on Strauss Street disappeared, and were replaced by sensational and commercial tabloids. A culture of materialism crept into our lives, exuding aggression, indulgent, unsatisfying and populist, supported by scientific method in the guise of economic theory. And I found myself part of the infrastructure that supports its existence.

I came to economics only because it serves as a workshop for pouring words from real life into formal models. I did not imagine that my professional work would touch upon questions of economic policy. For many years I considered problems of social injustice to be of far lesser consequence than the existential questions: Jewish identity, what it means to be Israeli, and Israel as an occupying nation. Eventually, when I began to think also about real-life economics, I realized that I had opinions on these issues too. However, my opinions have absolutely no relation to economics in its academic sense.

The economic system as a game

My favorite game as a child was Rikuz, the Zionist version of Monopoly. In Rikuz, you could build red houses and blue hotels, purchase remote communities, and control all of the capital of the electric and water companies. You could tour the country and even visit Hebron and Bethlehem, which were far beyond the border at the time. It was great fun to play the game during summer vacation, on the cool green floor of my bedroom.

There are many games that enable children to learn, exercise their imaginations and dream. How did we choose which game to play? We understood that chess is for deep thinkers, that Scrabble is for the fluent of tongue, and basketball is intended for the tall. Everyone liked a different game. We agreed on which game to play by balancing our conflicting desires, and because we wanted to stay friends.

I think of the choice of economic policy in the same way as I think of the childhood choice of which game to play.

There are many economic games that enable people to consume, produce, contribute to society, grow and prosper. Some economic games benefit the workers and some benefit the wealthy; some are beneficial to the elderly, and some to the young; some of the economic games are complicated and suitable only for the best minds, while some are simple and can be played by anyone. Most of us believe that the rules of the economic game should be fair, but there is no consensus on the concept of fairness. Is it fair to compensate people according to the fruit of their effort or according to the effort itself? Should the economic game give more to those who need more? Is it right for someone whose parents won a lot in the previous game to enjoy an advantage when it is his turn to participate in the next game?

In order to define the economic game, answers are needed to questions such as: Who are the players? How should we deal with redundant players? What moves are allowed? What should be done if a few players acquire a dominant position in the game? What can be owned and traded? Should we take into account the possibility that some players have limited ability to play the economic game? How flexible are the rules of the game? And what course of action should be taken when players opt out of the game completely?

A society must decide which economic game it will play. Those who favor the natural economic game, which is seemingly free and without rules, actually support an economic game with very rigid rules – the rules of the jungle. Economics, as an academic field, has little to say about the question of which game to play. I reject the term "the right economic game." The political system – through public discussion and the balancing of its citizens' conflicting desires – must decide how to formulate and enforce the rules of the economic game.

The players

The definition of a game begins by specifying the players. This is true for board games and equally applies to economic games. Nearly all public economic decisions are made at the national level. Therefore, the definition of the group of players in the economic game is almost identical to the definition of who qualifies to be a citizen in the state. Citizenship laws define the jurisdiction of the rules of the economic game, and also define the individuals whose welfare is taken into consideration when setting the rules of the game. True, it is possible to imagine a state that not only looks after the interests of its own citizens, but acts in accordance with the dictates of universal justice. But the overwhelming majority of us, even if we care about all human beings, feel a stronger commitment to the covenant with our fellow countrymen and members of our nation. We feel that the rules of the game should serve, first and foremost, the members of our own society, protect us from those outside of the society's borders and perhaps even enable us to grow stronger at the expense of other nations. Who is entitled to join the nation? Who will be excluded?

Who will be born into the covenant and who will not be born at all? These are difficult questions that have an enormous impact on the society in which we live and, of course, on its economy as well.

"Who are the players?" we ask, and must address the rules of acceptance for new members to our club. In other words, we are dealing with immigration policy. The immigration laws in Israel are both inclusive and exclusive. On the one hand, they do not enable non-Jews to join the club, and on the other, they mandate the absorption of anyone who is defined under Israeli law as a Jew. Israel has shouted for years: "*aliya!*" (Jewish immigration) and conducts a policy of encouraging immigration by anyone who claims a genetic connection, even a dubious one, to the Jewish people. Thus, Israel has absorbed church-going Christians only because the family name of one of their grandparents sounded Jewish, and has brought in groups of people who practiced traditions that somehow resembled Jewish ones. Bringing them to Israel was not motivated by universal humanitarian motives or aimed at building a culturally unique society. If we felt we were carrying the entire world on our shoulders, we would open the gates to refugees seeking entrance at our borders and would not expel people who had the misfortune to be born in lands devoid of hope and who found a future among us. If we intended to build a society with a common cultural foundation, we would have fenced ourselves off from others according to cultural distinctions rather than ethnic ones. When all is said and done, the guiding principle of our immigration policy is apologetically racial. The desire not to appear as racists led us to suffice with a requirement for a flimsy genetic connection to the Jewish people. In recent years, this policy has also brought some immigrants whose connection to the Jewish people is a weak one, whose commitment to Israeli society is limited, and whose contribution to the economy is minimal.

"Who are the players?" we ask, and contend with the question of policy regarding the birthrate. Israel has always acted according to an ethos of encouraging childbirth. We have glorified families with many children (called "blessed with children" in Hebrew) even as we realized that most of them would have meager resources. The roots of the birthrate policy can be traced to the instinct of refilling the ranks that arose in the wake of the Holocaust. However, this policy engendered a tragic situation: we are inundated with births only among the population groups that are in dire need of assistance from others. And the others who are supposed to support the children of those groups are not eager to do so, and it is hard to blame them.

"Who are the players?" we ask, and need to decide on the status of the temporary players – that is, we need to formulate a policy regarding foreign workers. In recent decades, many countries, including Israel, hastily brought in large numbers of foreign workers out of national greed. We treated them as if they were raw material. Employing them improved the situation of the middle and upper classes, who enjoyed cheap and submissive labor, but it worsened the situation of those who could only serve as unskilled workers, particularly in the sectors in which the foreign workers were employed. We did not want to regard the foreign workers as part of our society, but the avarice blinded us from seeing that sooner or later they, or their children, would indeed become part of our society.

There is a consensus in Israel that it is one of the most talented nations, if not the most talented in the world. However, the nation is not a well-defined entity. Not every collection of human beings, even if it lives close to the holy places, can lay claim to this title.

The policy of providing incentives for childbirth, the policy on foreign workers, and the immigration policy are changing Israeli society to a greater extent than the construction of a subway in Tel Aviv, the addition of thousands of teachers to the education system, or the building of a land bridge between Yemen and Cyprus. Encouraging childbirth among the weaker segments of society and actively promoting immigration through negative selection – while at the same time expecting constant growth in per capita GDP and an improvement in pupils' achievements in the schools – is an expression of national psychological repression. Per capita GDP, which economists regard as an index of a society's wealth, is "the value of the national product" divided by the number of people in the society – and the denominator, not only the numerator, affects the quotient.

Many moral and ideological considerations influence the decision about who will play our national economic game. This decision has absolutely nothing to do with insights derived from economics. An economist's words carry the same weight as anyone else's on these issues.

The redundant players

The time: tenth grade, perhaps eleventh grade. The place: near the Allenby military base in Jerusalem. The event: a day with the Gadna Youth Corps, devoted to intensive pre-military training. The counselor appoints two group leaders, who alternately choose children for their groups. The groups are supposed to form two lines. Each child, in turn, has to run to the tree several hundred meters away and back, and when he gets back, the next child in the line sets off. The air is full of adolescent excitement, two years before their army call-up. It is strange how much people care about their group winning, even when they are divided into groups arbitrarily, and by the next day will not remember who was in which group. This competition really did not suit me. I was not physically fit, suffered from a lack of motivation and hated all physical activity. The group leaders had good reason to believe that even social pressure would not push me to succeed in finishing the run. In other words, the group that was "lucky" to have me on its team would never win. It goes without saying that they chose me last, after all of the girls. I was an unwanted player.

Each person comes to the conventional model of the economic market with a "basket." There are consumption goods in the basket, as well as production inputs to manufacture other products, and an important commodity called **time**. Each person would like to receive as much as he can, while giving as little as he can. And the market determines the terms of exchange for all of the products. In the model, as in reality, people are not equal; some have many assets and others have few. It seems that at least in one commodity, time, we are all equal: each morning, we all wake up and have at our disposal a treasure of 24 hours. But even in this there is no equality. People differ in their ability to turn time into other desirable products. A good education system tries to rectify the inequality in the productive capacity of people. However, it is not at all clear that progress and education compensate for the innate differences between human beings. As a result of technological progress, it is no longer necessary to exploit tens of thousands of slaves to build pyramids. It is unnecessary to send millions of soldiers to attack an enemy, and we can get by without batteries of women bent over small sewing machines. Very many people have become redundant. The economic desires and needs of human beings can be fulfilled without these superfluous people.

In children's games, there are ways to get rid of superfluous players. The other children "forget" to invite to the game a boy who dreams of playing in the NBA but does not know where to shoot the ball. A player in the chess club who always loses and spoils the match is showered with ridicule until he keeps away. I quickly realized that it was best for me to keep away from sports.

In the economic game, the redundant players do not vanish. If they could migrate to another country where they would be less redundant, many of them would do so. But the option to migrate is very limited. The redundant are on the fringes of society, censured and blamed for their own unfortunate situation. Society calls upon them to break out of the cycle of unemployment through programs for professional retraining that they have no chance of completing. They stand in endless lines to receive welfare benefits that are barely enough to sustain them. Some of them take consolation in the illusion that one day, things will be better, and if not for them, at least for their children. All this only hides a simple truth: we have no need for the redundant, they have no economic value. Economics has nothing to say about the question of how to contend with their redundancy.

Permissible actions

Every game has rules that define what is permissible and what is prohibited, who can do what and when. The rules of the game are intended to give each of the players an equal standing. Sometimes there is no alternative, and the rules create inequality among the participants. For example, someone has to play with the white pieces in chess and receives the advantage that white has over black. But even when the rules of the game do not discriminate the players, they have an impact in determining who will be the strong players in the game. If the rules of basketball allowed players to shove their opponents, the outstanding players would be like football heroes. If the rules of the game of chess prohibited the players from looking at the board and they needed to play by memory alone, a chess master with poor memory would become weak. If scrabble players were allowed to use a computer, the outstanding players would be Internet mavens rather than those with a rich vocabulary.

The rules of the economic game are heaped together in countless voluminous books of laws, regulations, rulings and administrative instructions. They are worded in a way that purports to place all players on an equal footing. But only ostensibly.

Take, for example, the players of the economic game called **entrepreneurs**. An entrepreneur chooses a business in which to invest his capital and energy. The decision whether to allow entrepreneurs to open manpower businesses is likely to affect the outcome of the economic game, and to be significant not only for the entrepreneur, but also for the workers and employers.

Let's consider the case of a female engineer who is interested in working if she can find someone to help her with the housework. Across the street lives a woman who can serve as a cleaning lady but cannot work as an engineer. It would be beneficial for everyone if the woman across the street devotes time to helping with the engineer's housework and, in exchange, receives some of the engineer's earnings. Two questions arise. First, how will the two women find each other? And second, what portion of the engineer's earnings should she give to the cleaning lady?

"Matchmaking" mechanisms create these matches: bulletin boards, employment bureaus, social connections or private intermediaries. The engineer will not publish an advertisement in the newspaper if cleaning ladies do not look at the Help Wanted ads, and the cleaning lady will not visit the employment bureau if potential employers do not turn to these bureaus to look for workers. If private individuals can open manpower agencies, an equilibrium might be created in which all of those involved, from both sides of the street, turn to a single manpower agency that operates in the area. In this equilibrium, the agent is in a position to charge a significant agent's fee as a condition for putting the engineer and the cleaning lady in touch with each other. The result is that the engineer's income will be divided not only between the engineer and the cleaning lady, but also with the agent.

What is wrong with this? First, a manpower agency is simply unnecessary. Ostensibly, it is a service that matches workers and employers. But the engineer and the cleaning lady can easily be matched via other means: bulletin boards, community centers, employment bureaus and the Internet. The problem of suitability is not a complicated one in the case of cleaning ladies, and the nature of the relationship depends mainly on their meeting in person. The entrepreneurs make a profit not because of their contributions to others, but because they position themselves on the bridge between employers and employees. Second, for various reasons manpower agencies in this market give preference to the employers' interests over those of the workers. The result is not only that they eat into the wages of the cleaning lady. They also influence the outcome of the negotiation between the engineer and the cleaning lady and prevent the cleaning lady from benefiting from her economic power even when there is a shortage of cleaning ladies in the market. Most remarkable are the importers of foreign workers, who bring them to Israel and often collect fees that are equivalent to a year's wages – a fee greatly out of proportion with the expenses involved in arranging their transfer from their home countries to their place of employment. When there is a severe shortage of foreign workers, the manpower agencies separate the demand and supply sides, and ensure that the shortage in workers is translated into an increase in their profits rather than a raise in the workers' wages.

Other entrepreneurs mediate between workers and employers, presenting themselves as service contractors. They sell a product called home cleaning without citing the identity of the worker who will do the work. Instead of employing the worker directly, the engineer contacts the contractor who provides her with the submissive worker. The contractor relieves the engineer of the headache of employing the worker, as well as of any guilt feelings about the fact that the wage is below the minimum wage. During the past decades, one can find these service contractors almost everywhere. Public and private entities have grown tired of employing cleaning personnel, gardeners and security guards directly ("Who has the patience to deal with them?"), and they employ these workers via a service contractor whose main job is to make sure that the worker's salary and status remain low – for the benefit of their clients and their own profits.

The rules of the economic game must determine which moves are permissible for these talented entrepreneurs who have the knack of identifying business opportunities. Just as the government prohibits touting movie tickets, it could prevent entrepreneurs from acting as middlemen between workers and employers. At the same time, just as the government is committed to issuing currency notes, it is obliged to operate a public employment service that connects workers and employers in a simple and efficient way, without nibbling away a piece of the pie.

No, I do not think that the government should provide matchmaking services in all economic areas. In the luxury housing market, for example, the estate agents share information with the buyers and sellers, thus facilitating activity in the market. There is less risk of estate agents prejudicing the outcome of the bargaining because the buyers and sellers in the luxury housing market have more or less equal capabilities. Sometimes the market players are on the side of the seller and sometimes on the side of the buyer. Government intervention in this market is redundant because it would not prevent or correct injustice, or improve the efficiency of dealing in this market.

The employment conditions of workers at the lower end of the scale have received some public attention in recent years, and a number of regulations have been introduced that slightly enhance the standing of these workers in the economic game. It was not professional economists who generated this change. Even after legislative reforms, these workers remained powerless and transparent in the workplaces where they scrub, garden and guard. In the future too, the weak may find more consolation in poems than in the discussion papers of economists.

The problem of wealth

Every few years, the world of children revolves around cards with pictures of cartoon heroes, sports champions or weapons of war. In schoolyards, children gather with the cards they purchased at the nearby kiosk. The children repeatedly play a particularly simple game that ends with the loser surrendering one card to the winner. The children also trade the cards according to a price system determined in the children's market and expressing the rarity of the cards. All is peaceful until one morning a child comes to school whose parents treated him to a large number of cards. The child's pockets bulging with cards arouse great envy, not only among the children who have no cards at all, but also among the "middle class," who have just a few. Occasionally, he graciously gives a card or two to a child he wants to be nice to or as protection money to the class bully. This is sufficient to win him an exalted status in the society of children. But one day, the "exalted one" goes outside during the recess and forgets his cards in his satchel. When he returns to the classroom, he screams. The cards have disappeared.

Game designers assume that players want to win. But winning is not always players' only objective. There are chess players who do not want to take advantage of a blunder by their opponent and allow the opponent to take back a foolish move, even when this means giving up a sure victory. There are sprinters who are mainly interested in their time, and would rather come last in a race against champions than win against poor opposition. But some players also have less positive objectives: those who not only want to win, but to win again and again, and to do so in a big way, in order to feel the intoxication of superiority over their rivals, that gives them status and power.

The accepted model in economics assumes that people are interested in enjoying as much as possible: bread, books, health services and living space. Money is intended to be a means of exchange for obtaining goods and has no intrinsic worth. In the economic game, however, people have desires beyond the aspiration to increase their consumption basket. Some of these desires are beneficial to others. There are merchants who do not feel comfortable exploiting a mistake by another party to a transaction. Some employers feel they should pay a decent wage to their workers, above the market price. But there are problematic desires too. One such example is the desire of very wealthy people to become very, very wealthy. This only involves a small number of people, but these few can determine the fate of many other people. If they become even more affluent, this will only have a marginal impact on their consumption. Even Bill Gates does not eat more than five eggs a day and cannot travel simultaneously in two private jets. Extremely affluent people long for greater wealth, but not in order to get more consumer goods. Success itself is what enchants them. Some of them enjoy being able to share their wealth with others; some of them crave the power of control over those who are subject to their authority and benevolence.

Many countries suffer from the problem of wealth – that is, the concentration of great wealth (and therefore, great power) in the hands of a few. What is wrong with this? We do not want a class of aristocrats to control our lives, regardless of how small and enlightened this group might be. Concentration of wealth is anti-democratic because the idea of democracy does not only mean conducting elections every four years, but also aspiring to distribute political power equally between all citizens. Whoever is not worried about oligarchy, whoever does not want to take responsibility and make an impact, whoever prefers that others determine his way of life – must hope that the wealthy elite turns out to be a community of angels who do not abuse their power.

The damages caused by the concentration of wealth can be seen in the daily evidence of tycoons wielding influence over public figures and the media, the takeover of public assets through the exploitation of wealth, and the use of wealth for political purposes. Even philanthropy, the charitable aspect of wealth, is not necessarily as welcome as it seems. When a society assigns authority to philanthropists, it also leaves them to set the priorities. For example, as a result of generous donations received, the universities develop in directions that are far from being the result of academic considerations and national priorities. Some of the salient changes in academia and in cultural institutions have expressed the priorities of tycoons interested in commemorating themselves and their relatives on the walls of buildings. And these refined individuals prefer quasi-academic areas rather than the faculties of arts and science.

The problem of poverty is urgent and cries out for attention. The problem of wealth is less obvious, but threatens to transform democracy into a mere formality. From one perspective, it is easier to address the problem of poverty because it involves giving, while dealing with the problem of wealth requires taking. People get angry when they do not receive something they feel is due to them, but they are very, very angry when something they already possess is taken from them. Let's look at the inheritance tax, for example. It is the most just tax I know. It is so just that there would be justification for it even if the government did not collect taxes at all. Inheritance tax dilutes the concentration of capital in the hands of the few. The tax is only slightly detrimental to the system of incentives that encourages people to conduct useful economic activity. Nonetheless, and despite the fact that inheritance tax is imposed in nearly all of the countries we envy, there is enormous opposition to instituting this tax in Israel. The tax is perceived by most people, including those who are not affluent, as crueler than income tax. This is because income tax takes something that is not yet owned, while inheritance tax takes a bite out of something that has already found a home among a person's assets.

Economic models generally ignore the aspiration of individuals to gain power and control over other people. The problem of wealth is not a topic of discussion in the customary economic discourse.

Assets

The rules of the game specify what each player holds at the beginning of the game. In chess, each player starts the game with 16 pieces ready to capture and eliminate the other player's pieces. At the beginning of the game of Monopoly, most of the assets are in the bank. The players receive banknotes throughout the game. They can accumulate the banknotes or convert them to properties, houses, hotels or railroads at prices set in advance by the designer of the game. Players cannot take a coin from their pocket and add it to the game. The houses are not tradable between the players, and you cannot take a loan from the bank.

In the economic game too, someone (the state, who else...) must decide which assets the players can play with. We are familiar with the idea of a commune, in which all of the property belongs to the collective; the collective not only decides the fate of the material assets, but also decides what work each individual will do, what he will eat and what he will wear. On the other hand, in the completely free market, a person can sell himself into slavery, his body for prostitution and his body parts for transplants. Between a commune, where there is no place for private ownership, and an economic system in which every object belongs to someone and everything is tradable, there is a broad range of possibilities. In order for ownership to have validity, the community must recognize it and it must be backed by an enforcement authority. The designer of the economic game is the one who determines which assets can be owned, which assets are tradable, which assets will be under the state's control and which will be privately owned.

I think that most of us believe that it is appropriate for a person to own what he has produced with his own two hands and that a person has a right to trade what he has produced in exchange for something else. Most of us also believe that a person's ownership of his body should be protected and should not be an object of commerce; that parks and beaches should not be in private hands. Beyond these principles, the issues are controversial.

I understand the revulsion felt in light of the revelations of corruption and waste in the public service, revulsion that feeds the enthusiasm for the privatization process, which is essentially a transfer of control over assets from public to private hands. But the sale of a bank to a businessman does not ensure its efficient operation and certainly does not improve its business ethics. Before a government company is privatized, the appointment of a crony as CEO is liable to result in a criminal indictment. After the privatization, the appointment of a party activist favored by the controlling owner is considered to be his right.

True, it is problematic to assign too many tasks and authorities to the state. The government is too large an entity, with an abundance of missions and a narrow-topped pyramid structure. Leaders, like tycoons, sometimes use their power – and not necessarily for the good. I also believe that it would be best for us if the government focuses on governing rather than managing. The government should concentrate on defining and enforcing the rules of the economic game and not engage in the ongoing management of matters that others can execute without fear of harming the public interest. But removing control of the nation's assets from government hands does not require converting them into private, fully tradable assets. In order to address the problem of wealth, the concept of ownership of assets of special public interest could be defined in a way that restricts the use that can be made of them. For example, we could require that the ownership of such assets be distributed between a large number of individuals, or that a government company that passes into private hands be managed with extra consideration for the welfare of the employees.

Assets can be outside of government control and still not under private ownership. Authority could be divided between the government and a public non-governmental entity that manages the nation's assets. The directors of the Public Economy Authority could be elected by the founder shareholders – that is, all of the citizens of the state – rather than being appointed by the government. It is not absurd that citizens would not only elect their leaders but also the directors of this Authority. (In the U.S., the attorneys general are also elected by the public.) The director must be a person of integrity, with managerial attributes. He should be committed only to the public that elected him and will perhaps reelect him, and must consider not only the balance sheets of the Public Economy Authority, but also the Authority's level of service and how it treats its employees.

Of the assets that individuals can accumulate, land is the best candidate for expropriation. The Bible was familiar with this notion too. The economic significance of the idea of the jubilee year is that land is to be held by individuals for a limited period and is eventually redistributed among all. Land is also a unique asset in the high-tech era, a sought-after treasure that is dwindling quickly and which cannot be smuggled abroad or imported without wars. Leaving land in public hands and only selling leasing rights would drastically reduce the problem of wealth without harming market activity. Even if the rules of the economic game do not permit the accumulation of land, people will continue to be exposed to enough incentives to work and exert themselves.

The question of ownership is discussed in economics, but the main economic discourse focuses on the efficiency of various ownership arrangements. In any case, it seems to me that the views of economists regarding the boundary between the public and private ultimately derive from emotional positions rather than scholarly conclusions. Some are wary of government and would like to hand the world over to the private sector, while others are outraged by tycoons and wish to strengthen the power of the state. I see nothing wrong with this. I do not see why economic models have a place in these matters and emotions do not.

The player's limitations

When we think in game theory about a game, we assume that the players have a perfect ability to play it. In tic-tac-toe, for example, it is reasonable to assume that each player prefers a victory to a tie, and prefers a tie to a defeat. Thus, we have a game with an absolute conflict of interests. Some will argue that if both players are rational, game theory proves that the outcome of the game is known in advance – a tie. This is because each player in the game has a strategy that ensures he will not lose, regardless of what his opponent does. Consequently, if the game does not end in a tie, at least one of the two players must have made a wrong move at least once, a move that led to a situation in which the other player could win.

But human beings are not perfect players. They make errors and do not always take advantage of opportunities. Despite the fact that tic-tac-toe is a well-known and simple game, not everyone is familiar with the strategies guaranteeing that a player will not lose in the game. This fact enables the game to survive. No one would be interested in participating in a game whose outcome is known in advance. The limited rationality of the players makes the game more interesting than it appears when analyzed via game theory. This also applies to other games. A game's outcome is likely to be unpredictable, even when we have a mathematical theorem stating that if the players act rationally, the outcome of the game is known in advance. The outcome of a game in the real world depends on the abilities of the players to play the game, i.e., their memory or logical ability, associative ability or manipulativeness.

Most of the players in the economic game have only limited familiarity with the economic game and make plenty of mistakes. Almost all of us have difficulty accepting rational decisions on substantial matters such as pension planning and health insurance. And, of course, most of us are unable to trade in derivatives on the markets in Chicago and Shanghai (if we even know what they are). Most economic players find it difficult to identify economic opportunities and respond to them. This is a problem for supporters of traditional economic thought, which assumes the existence of an unlimited number of entrepreneurs ready to jump at every opportunity that comes their way. A complex economic environment gives an advantage to speculative and manipulative players. The designers of the economic games tend to ignore the emotional and cognitive qualities required to excel at the game. I think the designers of board games are more sensitive to the personal qualities the game rewards and encourages.

The flexibility in the rules of the game

We all hated to lose in our childhood games. We were hurt, angry and kicked. Sometimes one of us would suddenly announce – that is, after realizing that the accepted version of the game was not working to his advantage – that we were actually playing a different version of the game. Usually it was the strong kid who made this declaration. We had no choice but to yield to him, to be angry and hold our tongues.

The players who are high up in the economic game, as enlightened as they pretend to be, aim to preserve their status and wealth. When market forces finally are about to benefit those who are lower down, someone announces that we are actually playing according to a different version of the game, one that ensures that everyone remains in their assigned places.

Here is an example: according to the rules of the economic game of the free market, occasional excesses of supply and demand affect prices, including the price of labor. The import of foreign workers in a particular industry affects the supply of labor and lowers the wages of those working (or who could have been working) in that industry. The movement of foreign workers is not determined only by market forces. We live in a village that is less global than it seems. Capital flows have become freer, but few people, even among those who champion the free market, would argue for the unregulated migration of labor. The designer of the economic game still sets entry quotas for foreign workers, even in states that practice economic liberalism. In order to comply with the principles of the free market, the designer must define a policy for importing workers in a particular industry that will depend on how critical the labor shortage is in that industry, and will ignore the status of those employed in it.

Indeed, for years there was a shortage of registered nurses, computer programmers and even economics professors in Israel, on the one hand, as well as of farm workers, caregivers and construction workers on the other. In conventional economic parlance, the added value to the economy of a worker in the first group of professions was higher than the added value of a worker in the second group. In all of these professions, there are very many foreign workers highly willing to come and work here for wages that are lower than those of Israeli workers. But we did not see plane loads of registered nurses and programmers at the airport, not to speak of economics professors. But we did see planes full of Thai workers, Filipino caregivers and Romanian construction workers. For years the state has permitted the entry of foreign workers in industries where local workers are not unionized and lack political power, and has refrained from doing this in industries with a well-organized work force, despite the fact that in those fields the contribution of foreign workers to the economy could have been greater.

So, when attorneys, accountants, economics professors or programmers are lucky and the demand for these professionals exceeds the supply, then it is all well and good for their wages to rise, as the free expression of market forces. But when it appears that luck is shining on those who are only capable of working as caretakers, and the surge in demand threatens to benefit them, pressures are exerted to make the rules of the game more flexible and allow the import of foreign workers, thus preventing the market forces from performing their role. I am not aware of any moral or economic justification for this absurdity. In order to understand how this occurs, there is no need to study economics. You just need to recall how the strong children changed the rules of the game when they were not to their liking.

Spoiling the game

Sometimes in children's games, a great drama is enacted, when some players abruptly quit in protest. This happens after some of the children are struck by a feeling that something is unfair to them. In the economic game we play, this type of abrupt exit from the game is also not a far-fetched scenario. Let's imagine that we have reached the (not so distant) moment when there is nothing left to privatize. The postal bank, hospitals, universities, prisons and television channels – all have been privatized. An oligarch who made his money on a soccer team and power plants in Sleazistan has completed the acquisition of the police. All of the nation's lands have been sold. Nature Day, which was once a festival of renewal, became the holiday of privatization, celebrating the victory of the forest over the wasteland, efficiency over bureaucracy, the private over the public.

But then some minor shareholders, who invested their money in the largest company in the state, discover that the company's chairman of the board has appointed his son, a famous ne'er-do-well, to manage a subsidiary company. These shareholders file a class-action suit against the company's defective management, claiming that the firm's obligation is to maximize its profits and not to pamper the well-born. This does not entail a criminal offense, so they cannot ask the police to get involved. The embittered shareholders are unable to prove that the appointment stemmed from extraneous interests, and the lawsuit is rejected.

Next, the shortage of land in the metropolitan area engenders a rumor that several tycoons from overseas have gained control of most of the valuable lands in the area, and are refusing to sell them, anticipating a rise in prices during the coming decade. At the same time, there is an unexpected water shortage, despite the fact that it has not been a particularly dry year. Someone on a popular television program claims that the privatized water companies have collaborated to cut back the supply of water in order to drive up its price. However, no one is watching the program because on the competing channel the reality show *A Director is Born* is being broadcast. Rumors are circulating that the value of pension funds' investments in Mongolian currency slumped after Mongolia's application to join the European Union was rejected, contrary to expectations. This leads to a new banking crisis.

The situation reaches a boiling point when a dirty bomb is discovered in the subway. The privatized market finds it difficult to cope with the catastrophe. Investors reach the conclusion that the idea of investing in this country is not only uneconomic, it is crazy.

At this stage, people begin to have a sneaking suspicion that perhaps we have gone too far. There is a growing realization among the public that privatization has transferred control of the society from the hands of elected politicians, who are subject to some sort of oversight, to other people who are no less infantile, who do whatever they want. Now, only one thing remains for the people of this country to do: to change the rules. Or, in other words – nationalize.

At best, there are only a lot of tears shed when the rules are changed in the economic game. It is really not very pleasant. Unlike privatization, nationalization hurts; and only when it occurs do we recall that the smartest way to prevent the cruelty of expropriation is to make it less easy to accumulate wealth. The economists I know do not discuss nationalization, at least not until very recently. For those who wish to be ahead of their time, I would advise putting aside their research plans and starting to discuss the question that will become more relevant – what to nationalize and how to go about it.

Almost the end

It is possible to discuss social and economic issues in an abstract way and to treat Israel like Finland and Thailand, as just another society whose members want to survive, plus a little bit more. But a fundamental problem makes Israel unique. The existence of the national home for the Jewish people in the Land of Israel has about as much economic logic as building a convalescent home on a traffic island. I use the word economic in the sense in which in recent years we have examined the need for public infant welfare clinics, the construction of the separation wall and the transition to alternative energies. Yes, it is possible to build a sanitarium on a traffic island. You just need to also build acoustic walls to block the noise, stop the traffic on the highway whenever a guest arrives, or (if this is not sufficient) completely close the highway. A convalescent home on a traffic island would disappear if our economic world were managed by the forces of the free market, which would move the convalescent home from the traffic island to the mountain forests.

Let the market forces operate over time without constraints and you will find that the Zionist project is foolhardy. Look at the members of this so-called talented nation, from the development towns to the *nouveaux riches* high-rises of Tel Aviv, and send them forth, from Manhattan to Silicon Valley, and you will receive a much more economically efficient outcome. And here's a thought that is not mere demagoguery. Israel's annual defense expenditure per average Jewish family in Israel would be enough to pay a year's rent on a fine home – four bedrooms, two baths and a garden – in Wisconsin. If you add the cost of investment in the West Bank settlements, you could also have a swimming pool.

Perhaps things would be different if we lived in a virtual Middle East in which Israel had peace with its neighbors and led the region to progress and prosperity. I am doubtful about the possibility of such an ideal space. According to both the Zionist left and the messianic right, the Jewish state is inherently separate and aloof.

Anyone who wants a Jewish state in the Land of Israel must accept the necessity of imposing limitations on the free economy. In order for Israel to exist, its citizens – particularly its most talented and mobile ones – must have a reason to live there even at a significantly lower standard of living than they could enjoy elsewhere. Some have a religious reason for this: the holiness of life in the Land of Israel. For the majority, this reason can be the language, or the unique culture, or ensuring the framework of strong solidarity that includes a commitment to the principles of the welfare state: ensuring a basic basket of services – in the fields of health, housing, education, security and law.

Adherence to the principles of the welfare state does not contradict the value of personal responsibility. I am not referring to the prime minister's personal responsibility to resign after embarking on an unnecessary war (though taking such personal responsibility would not hurt either), but rather the personal responsibility of the individual for himself and his family. Thus, for example, the Home Front Command must make sure that bomb shelters meet the required standards, but the maintenance of the shelters should be performed by the citizens who are slated to use them in time of trouble. The welfare bureau should care for broken families and for those who are alone in the world. But the elderly bedridden man from the north who has family in central Israel should be cared for during a rocket attack by his children, grandchildren and great-grandchildren, and not by officials from the municipality's welfare department. Ensuring a basic level of health for all citizens is one of the foundations of the welfare state, but the decision whether to devote financial resources today for costly, life-extending drugs tomorrow should be made by each individual for himself through insurance plans whose premiums are linked to income. Even if Israel continues to sanctify the Law of Return, the responsibility for absorbing new immigrants to Israel should be assumed by the immigrants themselves.

The concept of the welfare state reflects a set of values expressed in Israel's declaration of independence: "The State of Israel... will be based on freedom, justice and peace as envisaged by the prophets of Israel." And the prophets of Israel were not market economists. But I fear the worldview that demands exaggerated public responsibility for the individual. I am afraid that the group in society which is supposed to take care of others will not be able to carry the burden expected of it and will find refuge in right-wing economics. Perhaps we complain too much about society shirking its responsibility for the individual and too little about the individual's exaggerated expectations for society to protect him. Solidarity does not require patronage, and society's concern for the weak is not a license for evading personal responsibility. Exemption from personal responsibility is not efficient, is unfair and constitutes an imposition on others.

End

On one side of my room when I was a child stood a large dresser, with an alarm clock and my mother's sewing box perched on top of it. Inside the dresser was the forbidden drawer containing the secret letters and pictures that my mother and father kept from their parents' homes. Next to the dresser was a large bookcase containing an encyclopedia for the young, a world atlas, Edmondo De Amicis's *The Heart*, and several other books that I read over and over again. Along the walls, opposite each other, were two iron beds with squeaky springs. On the other side of the room, opposite the dresser, stood a desk that faced a three-leaf window and two large, green trees that protected me from the southern sun and caressed me on summer days. Even now, when I think of an exciting moment that occurred not long ago while sitting at a desk – thinking, writing or speaking on the phone – I imagine myself sitting at that desk from my childhood and looking out through the window at the two trees.

Between this bedroom furniture, my soccer field stretched across the floor of the room. The field was a matrix of green tiles, twelve tiles long and nine tiles wide. When I discovered in the encyclopedia that the dimensions of a regulation soccer field are 120 meters long and 90 meters wide, my soccer field became perfect. The goal posts were red-topped, lacquered wooden pins, remnants of a children's bowling set I received as a gift from neighbors on the day my sister celebrated her *bat mitzvah*. Two large Lego pieces represented the two teams. A blue Lego piece was the Israeli national team and a red, green or yellow one represented the foreign team. The ball was a small Lego piece. I would hold the two large Lego pieces in my hands, dribble, pass, kick, block, miss and score on behalf of all twenty-two players. The Israeli national team included all of the stars of the period, with one exception: I played in place of one of the forwards. And I was also Nehemiah Ben Avraham, the legendary Israeli sports announcer who broadcast all major matches, and now also those from the stadium on the floor. I could not remember the real names of the players on foreign teams, so the lineup of the rival teams was always: Ig (goalkeeper), Big and Gig (defenders), Dig, Vig and Zig (midfielders), and Hig, Tig, Kig, Lig and Mig (forwards). When a goal was scored, the roar of the crowd escaped my lips in a whisper, because the game was top secret and no-one could watch it. When someone was about to enter the room, I would hide the Lego pieces between the clumps of fluff under the dresser and stand with the feigned innocence of someone who has something to conceal. During most of the game, the rival team was ahead and held a 3:0 lead in the final minutes. But then, an unknown forward (that is, I) would score four goals to win a great victory for the team in blue.

I would immerse myself in this game almost every day, even when I was already in high school. In fact, perhaps I am still playing the same game. The room became lecture halls and academic journals. The Lego pieces became the players in the formal models. I realized that the green floor was an imaginary world that enabled me to do what I could not do in the real game in the neighborhood. Standing by the podium, I realize that the models I deal with in economics are fables. The games on the cold floor did not help me play soccer and the economic models have not helped me formulate views on social issues. Everything, for better or worse, comes from those green tiles and remains there.

Bibliographical Notes

The results of the experiments reported in chapters 1, 2 and 4 rely on the data collected via my Internet site: http://gametheory.tau.ac.il. Some of the results were published in: Ariel Rubinstein, "Instinctive and Cognitive Reasoning: A Study of Response Times", *Economic Journal*, 117 (2007), 1243–59. All of my publications are available to read and download from my webpage:

http://arielrubinstein.tau.ac.il/

Introduction

In the sections *Economics and Me*, *Economic Tales* and *Tellers of Tales*, I drew from my lecture "Micro-economic Theory: Miracles or Wonders", The Israeli Academy of Sciences (December 1995).

The comparison of an economic model to a tale is based on the discussion in: Ariel Rubinstein, "Dilemmas of an Economic Theorist", *Econometrica*, 74 (2006), 865–83. See also: Robert Lucas, "What Economists Do", Unpublished Manuscript, University of Chicago (1988).

The illustration on page 17 is from *Fairy Tales and Other Stories* by Hans Christian Anderson (Humphrey Milford: Oxford University Press, 1914).

The economic model on page 18 is from my article "Perfect Equilibrium in a Bargaining Model", *Econometrica*, 50 (1982), 97–110. The Bargaining Tale is also based on this article.

The source of Hotelling's main street model is: Harold Hotelling, "Stability in Competition", *The Economic Journal*, 39 (1929), 41–57.

The Tale of the Three Tailors was part of a lecture delivered in Israel under various names (for example: "Comments on the Failure of Competitiveness" and "Equality and Prosperity in Israeli Society").

Chapter 1

The discussion about the response to the epidemic example is based on: Amos Tversky and Daniel Kahneman, "Rational Choice and the Framing of Decisions", *Journal of Business*, 59 (1986), 261–78.

The example of the lost ticket is taken from: Daniel Kahneman and Amos Tversky, "Choices, Values, and Frames", *American Psychological*, 39 (1984), 341–50.

The pen example is from: Itamar Simonson and Amos Tversky, "Choice in Context: Tradeoff Contrast and Extremeness Aversion", *Journal of Marketing Research*, 29 (1992), 281–95.

The camera example is similar to examples that appear in the following two papers: Joel Huber, John Payne and Christopher Puto, "Adding Asymmetrically Dominated Alternatives: Violations of Regularity and the Similarity

Hypothesis", *Journal of Consumer Research*, 9 (1982), 90–98; and Eldar Shafir, Itamar Simonson and Amos Tversky, "Reason-Based Choice", *Cognition*, 49 (1993), 11–36.

The example of the dice is taken from: Amos Tversky and Daniel Kahneman, "Extensional versus Intuitive Reasoning", *Psychological Review*, 91 (1984), 293–315.

Chapter 2

The initial part of this chapter is taken from a lecture entitled "John Nash, Beautiful Mind and Game Theory," which I presented in twelve places during the period 2002–2007.

Sylvia Nasar's book cited here is: *A Beautiful Mind* (New York: Simon & Schuster, 1998). See also: Sylvia Nasar, "The Lost Years of a Nobel Laureate", *The New York Times* (13 November 1994).

The Traveler's Dilemma is taken from: Kaushik Basu, "The Traveler's Dilemma: Paradoxes of Rationality in Game Theory", *American Economic Review*, 84 (1994), 391–95.

The treasure game is discussed in: Ariel Rubinstein, Amos Tversky and Dana Heller, "Naïve Strategies in Competitive Games", in *Understanding Strategic Interaction: Essays in Honor of Reinhard Selten*, ed. by Wulf Albers, Werner Güth, Peter Hammerstein, Benny Moldovanu and Eric van Damme (New York: Springer-Verlag, 1996), pp. 394–402.

The following books and articles are also mentioned in this chapter:

Avinash Dixit and Barry Nalebuff, *Thinking Strategically: The Competitive Edge in Business, Politics and Everyday Life* (New York: Norton, 1993).

John McMillan, *Games, Strategies, and Managers* (Oxford: Oxford University Press, 1992).

John Nash, Nobel Autobiography: http://nobelprize. org/nobel_prizes/economics/laureates/1994/nashautobio. html

John Nash, "Non-Cooperative Games", *Annals of Mathematics*, 2nd Ser., 54 (1951), 286–95.

John von Neumann and Oskar Morgenstern, *Theory of Games and Economic Behavior* (Princeton: Princeton University Press, 1944).

Chapter 3

The presentation of the jungle economy in this chapter is based on the article: Michele Piccione and Ariel Rubinstein, "Equilibrium in the Jungle", *Economic Journal*, 117 (2007), 883–96.

In its initial version, the chapter was presented in a lecture entitled, "Introduction to the Jungle Economy", Tel Aviv University (May 2003).

The proof of the existence of competitive equilibrium is from David Gale and was published in the article: Lloyd Shapley and Herbert Scarf, "On Cores and Indivisibility", *Journal of Mathematical Economics*, 1 (1974), 23–37.

Chapter 4

The beginning of the chapter is based on a lecture I delivered to the Israeli Sociological Society in February 2001.

The chapter draws from the article: Jacob Glazer and Ariel Rubinstein, "On the Pragmatics of Persuasion: A Game Theoretical Approach", *Theoretical Economics*, 1 (2006), 395–410.

For more on pragmatics, see: Paul Grice, *Studies in the Way of Words* (Cambridge, MA: Harvard University Press, 1989).

Chapter 5

This chapter is in part based on my following articles (all available from my personal webpage http://arielrubinstein.tau.ac.il/):

"On the Problem of Wealth", *Haaretz*, 18 December 2003.

"The Day after Privatization", *Yedioth Ahronoth*, 12 February 2007.

"A World in Which Many People are No Longer Useful" (Viviane Forrester's "The Economic Horror"), *Haaretz Books*, 20 March 2002.

"Six Thoughts on Economics and Society" in *The Root of the Matter*, ed. by Rubik Rosenthal (Jerusalem: Keter, 2005).

"On Personal Responsibility", *Calcalist*, 18 February 2008.

Acknowledgements

Many people assisted me. Eli Zvuluny, Dina Zafriri, Dan Raveh, Yehudah Meltzer, Yuval Salant, Michal Yafet, Noga Dim, Uzi Segal, Adi Raveh, Kobi Glazer, Rani Spiegler, Tair Shachner-Rochman and Tami Chapnik-Harel contributed with their comments. Eli Zvuluny built the book's website. Yanek Yuntaf designed the cover of the original edition. Thank you all.

Many thanks to the two who were involved in the translation process: Ira Moskowitz and Alan Hercberg.

Special thanks go to two people:

To Alma Cohen-Vardi, the editor of the original Hebrew edition of the book, who treated the text gently, corrected and improved it with unfailing patience.

To Ayala Arad, who accompanied the writing of the book with wise advice, incisive criticism and words of encouragement.

This book does not end here...

At Open Book Publishers, we are changing the nature of the traditional academic book. The title you have just read will not be left on a library shelf, but will be accessed online by hundreds of readers each month across the globe. We make all our books free to read online so that students, researchers and members of the public who can't afford a printed edition can still have access to the same ideas as you.

Our digital publishing model also allows us to produce online supplementary material, including extra chapters, reviews, links and other digital resources. Find *Economic Fables* on our website to access its online extras. Please check this page regularly for ongoing updates, and join the conversation by leaving your own comments:

http://www.openbookpublishers.com/product/136

If you enjoyed the book you have just read, and feel that works like this should be available to all readers, regardless of their income, please recommend our titles to libraries and other readers, make a donation or sponsor a book. Our company is run entirely by academics, and our publishing decisions are based on intellectual merit and public value rather than on commercial viability. We do not operate for profit and all the revenue we generate is used to finance new Open Access publications.

For further information about what we do, how to donate to OBP, additional digital material related to our titles or to order our books, please visit our website.

OpenBook Publishers

Knowledge is for sharing

Lightning Source UK Ltd.
Milton Keynes UK
UKOW041942091012

200301UK00014B/54/P